RAISING A LEADER FOR LIFE

A Master Plan for Being an Intentional Parent

by CHRISTINA NEWBERRY
and OLIVIA RODRIGUEZ

DEDICATION

To my husband, Jeff,
You are the best daddy in the world
And to my grandchildren,
Every word was written
With you in my heart and on my mind

Published by *Leaders for Life Enterprises.*
Creating true leaders from the inside out across cultures and generations who will inspire change in their world.

Visit us at www.raisingleadersforlife.com or on Facebook at https://www.facebook.com/raisingleadersforlife/.

Cover design and layout by Brandy Egli

© 2018 by Christina Newberry

TABLE OF CONTENTS

PART ONE:
PREPARE FOR THE JOURNEY

INTRODUCTION — 9

- 1: Keep the End in Mind — 11
- 2: Be Grateful for the Grind — 21
- 3: Avoid Those Dangerous Detours and Distractions — 39

PART TWO:
ALL ABOARD

- 4: Identify Your Location — 57
- 5: Choose Your Traveling Companions — 73
- 6: Set the Climate Control — 89
- 7: Avoid the Potholes — 103
- 8: Welcome Mistakes — 115

PART THREE:
A TRIP OF A LIFETIME

- 9: Launch a Confident Leader — 129
- 10: Launch a Compassionate Leader — 149
- 11: Launch an Authentic Leader for Life — 159

ACKNOWLEDGMENTS — 165

ABOUT THE AUTHORS — 169

PART ONE

PREPARE FOR THE JOURNEY

INTRODUCTION

There's nothing worse than getting lost on a trip, especially when you're trying to get somewhere by a specific time. Anxiety raises, patience wanes, and frustration sets in. You might even snap a little too easily at the people traveling with you. Yet what a difference a map can make!

Parenting is also a journey. It's an especially long journey if you feel lost, and nearly every parent feels lost at some time or another. My hope is that this book will serve as a much-needed map for you. If you lessen your frustration, capture a vision, know what you're working towards AND how you can get there, you'll have less anxiety, more patience, and a new level of confidence.

It's always best to start a trip knowing where you a going. In this journey called parenting, you're traveling to meet your family's needs in the best possible way. Your family may have lots of needs, but your child has only one: you. Your child needs you to lead, love, and listen well. That's what being an intentional parent is all about, and it's what will make you a hero in your family's story.

I write about parenting from two primary lenses. First as a parent who is just finishing up guiding three children into adulthood. I made plenty of mistakes along the way and my hope is to help you not make the same ones. I also write from a martial arts perspective. I've been teaching martial arts for over thirty years. As the owner of two martial arts academies, I believe children thrive best when they are thought of as "leaders in training." When we intentionally parent our "leaders in training," it builds confidence and discipline while empowering our child to live a life of success as an adult. There's also actually a third lens I write from, and that's a faith perspective. While I want this book to be a book that anyone can read regardless of where they stand on issues of faith, my life has been changed by Jesus in such a profound way that occasionally it just leaks out. I commit to you that regardless of where you sit on the faith spectrum, you'll feel completely comfortable reading the words on these pages. That's very important to me.

I didn't write this book alone. My former student turned teacher and friend, Olivia Rodriguez, has been my partner in the journey. While both of us have contributed to the words on these pages, you'll hear only one voice: mine. We believe it will be an easier read for you that way.

At the end of every chapter you'll find a "Let's Be Intentional" section. This is designed to help you to take the concepts discussed in the chapter and apply them to your family. You may be tempted to skip over this section, but I want to encourage you to take the time to do the exercises. Too often we parent *reactively* rather than *proactively*. Doing the exercises will help you be proactive about leading your child.

> Can you see your child's future?

My passion is to create leaders for life. Imagine what our children's future will look like when their generation is equipped with the tools to become authentic, confident leaders. Can you see it? Will you join me in raising up a generation of leaders for life? If you are up for the challenge, turn the page so we can take this journey together.

1 Keep the End in Mind

I remember it like it happened yesterday. My doorbell rang and as I opened the door I found my next-door neighbor, Samantha, standing outside. I could tell she had been crying. "What's going on?" I asked. "I'm so upset," she said as she broke down in tears. "Mary just told me that she's made her decision about college. I had hoped she would stay in town and attend the University of Illinois. She, however, has decided to go out-of-state."

Her heart broke as she thought of her daughter moving so far away and being completely on her own. Even more concerning was the knowledge that the college Mary had chosen was known to be a real "party" school. My neighbor feared that her daughter was going there to party and would not take her academics seriously.

"I'm so sorry." I responded with a hug as I continued to listen to my friend pouring her heart out. In fact, we were together most of that day. We moved to the back yard to garden but it seemed our minds couldn't move past the topic of my friend's house being empty for the first time in over 30 years. Both of us quietly dug in the dirt, deep in thought as the weather changed from sunny to stormy, reflecting what seemed to be going on in our hearts.

I didn't realize it until later, but Samantha actually gave me a gift that day. You see, my own girls were two years behind hers. As I helped her process her pain, I took note and decided to make some parenting changes myself before my girls would be leaving home.

In fact, after my day with Samantha, I began to live each day with that end in mind.

That's what I hope this book is for you: a gift. I always tell my children, "let my years become your days," meaning that I hope they can learn from the years of experience and mistakes I have made, and use their time to explore new heights that I couldn't reach on my own. This is my hope for you.

I want this book to be your "Samantha." A straightforward perspective on parenting from someone who has been through what you are about to go through, and the real-life ups and downs about things I wish I had known when I was younger. Whether you are expecting, running around with toddlers, or managing a teenager, it is my hope that with this new vantage point, you will be able to increase your level of influence in the time you have remaining raising your children.

You Can't Get It Back

I suppose introductions are in order. My husband Jeff and I have three daughters. Our oldest is Melanie; Tiffany is our middle, and our youngest is Destani. Destani is eleven years younger than Melanie and nine years younger than Tiffany. You would think Destani had a different set of parents, and in a sense, she does. We are not the same parents that raised the first two; furthermore, the world is not the same in which they grew up.

About two years from my day with Samantha, it was time for our family to attend the World Championship Taekwondo Tournament in Little Rock, Arkansas. We loaded the car and hit the road, just as we had done for the past two-and-a-half decades. Nothing was out of the ordinary. We drove the 7 hours, attended the seminars, and participated in the competition. I thought this year was the same as all the other years, but I was wrong.

While I didn't know it then, this was the tournament where both of my girls would find the loves of their lives. Melanie met Seth, and Tiffany met Cesar. When we loaded up the car on the way home, I didn't realize how rapidly my family's life would change over the next few years. After two years of long-distance dating, my girls got married six months apart from each other, to these handsome, servant-hearted leaders I now call my sons.

Now let me tell you, that journey of letting go was bittersweet. I felt excited to see them so happy. Yet I felt pain in my heart to see them separating from our family and moving away to create their own families.

I would like to tell you that those two years were smooth sailing and I adjusted without a hiccup. But honestly, it took me a while. As my girls entered their young adult years they became my best friends, and at the time, my business partners of sorts. When they chose to get married so young, it left a big hole in my heart because I thought I would have more years with them at home.

Our family dynamic changed fast after the two oldest got married, and it was an adjustment for all of us. Destani went through an interesting transition from being the youngest to feeling like an only child. Here we are ten years later and in just a few months she will graduate from high school and I'll get to go through the whole process of letting go all over again.

During these years of change, I heard lovely advice from people who cared about me and had gone before me. However, I didn't always want to hear their comforting words: "You're gaining two sons, not losing two daughters." "Everyone goes through these feelings." "Your sadness will pass."

While my head knew all the words to be true, my heart didn't think these words were much comfort. I honestly didn't want to hear them, but I knew I needed the wisdom. Of course, now in hindsight I see that I gained two amazing son-in-laws who have helped me see that my girls made great choices. I am now blessed with an even larger family and two beautiful granddaughters.

> *It's never too late to make a next right step!*

Someday you'll also be looking at the child-raising years in the rear-view mirror. I'm sure on some days you long for it! But on other days, you're sentimental or even wracked with guilt over where you feel like you're failing. Yet the choices you make today as a parent can make the difference in how you see things in that rear-view mirror.

It's never too late to make a next right step! I want to help you look back, smile at the memories, and give grace for the mistakes. More than anything, however, I want to help you use whatever time you have left with your kids at home to its fullest.

Welcome to the Bleacher Seats

It was a Tuesday morning, several years into my season of parenting adult children that I met my Dad for breakfast. For the longest time I sat there in silence, staring out the window. "What's wrong, Bug?" my Dad asked, using his old nickname for me.

"Oh, I'm thinking about Tiffany." I had just come back from visiting my middle daughter in Texas and she seemed depressed after the birth of her second child. "I'm not sure she and Cesar are going to get the help they need. I'm also not sure its my place to voice this concern." My dad listened as I shared my concerns and then he offered this wise comment, "Welcome to the bleacher seats."

"What's that, dad?" I asked. "That's how I think of parenting adult children. You go from the role of coaching your children to being in the spectator section," Dad explained.

"Oh wow. That feels about right, Dad." He was really onto something. His words put my feelings into perfect perspective for me. As I look back on my journey as a parent, I see the truth in his description. A parent's job is to work themselves out of a job. From the very first day our children are born, our role is to create a mature, responsible adult.

For years, my personal parenting mission statement has been this: My role is to nurture a human being who is independent from the negative influences of life and dependent only on the love of God. This helped me remember what I was working towards. After chatting with my Dad, I realized it is okay and perfectly normal for me to move to the bleacher seats. It means I did my best, launched my children into life as confident adults, and get to enjoy the next phase of this incredible journey called parenting.

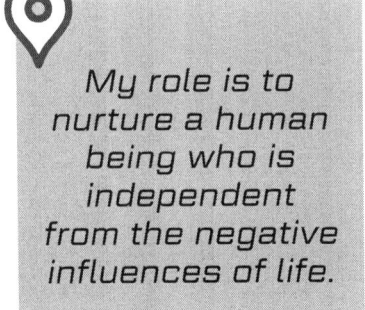

> My role is to nurture a human being who is independent from the negative influences of life.

That doesn't mean it's easy. It just means it's normal. Letting go is a regular part of the journey. However, letting them fly is much easier when you know they're fully equipped for life's challenges.

This means parenting intentionally with a finished picture as our everyday goal.

Parenting with the End in Mind

Have you heard Stephen Covey's phrase, "Prior planning prevents poor performance?" Well I have my own version: *Prior Planning Prevents Panicked Parents*. What if we parented every day with the end in mind? I once attended a leadership seminar where the facilitator took us through an exercise of identifying a dream we had and turning it into a goal we want to accomplish. Then we worked backwards to find out what steps needed to take place in order for that dream to become a reality.

This kind of exercise is powerful. It forces you to evaluate what steps will take you where you want to go and helps you identify any changes that need to be made. You can also determine what unnecessary distractions might take you off course.

In a similar way, we can evaluate the direction our parenting is taking our children and see what changes we want to make. Think about these questions: What will be running through your mind when your children leave the house? What do you want your child to know before they transition to adulthood? Thinking ahead, what characteristics do you want to define your relationship with your adult kids?

I'll go first. Remember when I said I made some adjustments after my day with Samantha? That day was a real wake-up call. First I thought about practical things, like how important it was to know how to change the oil in their car, how to travel safely across the country, and how to manage their money. While we're at it, do they know not to wash the red towels with the white towels?

Then my brain moved past basic practical skills to leadership and life skills. I wanted them to be confident in themselves. Have the ability to communicate well. Manage their feelings and emotions with maturity. I wanted them to have the courage to speak up for themselves and to stand up for injustice. I wanted them to understand compassion, to make good choices in friendships, and know how to find mentors to help them continually grow.

Of course there were even more of the "end product" characteristics that I thought about, but you see where I was going. Suddenly I had a picture in my mind of what I wanted to work towards for the next two years. This was my dream and now I just had to work backwards to find the steps to take in order for that dream to become a reality.

We Are Not Raising **Children**; We Are Raising **WORLD CHANGERS**

When we parent with intentionality and lead our kids with the end in mind, we are preparing them to thrive in their own little corner of the world. To make a difference. To stand strong when necessary. To show compassion where it's desperately needed. We're not just raising our kids to be adults, we're raising our kids to be world changers!

Think about this: the whole landscape of our country will be changed by our children's generation. This means as parents we have a big, challenging, and exciting job to do! What if we really believed our child could become the next president, the next Bill Gates, or the doctor who finds a cure for cancer? I'm not suggesting we put the weight of the world or our expectations on our children's shoulders, but I am suggesting that our child's potential is limitless.

If we are going to raise world changers, let's parent with the belief and expectation that our children can change the world with something as small as a smile or as great as a groundbreaking scientific discovery. With that vision in mind, the possibilities are endless and we can now start looking at the practical steps to wisely use our time with the kids at home. My commitment to you is to share both my victories and my mistakes as a parent of three and a mentor of many. I will give you hard-earned wisdom that will help you intentionally raise a leader for life. More than anything, I will provide the much-needed motivation to make every day count.

Let's Be Intentional

1. In this chapter, I gave you my personal "parenting mission statement." (My role is to nurture a human being who is independent from negative influences of life and dependent only on the love of God.) What might your parenting mission statement be?

   _____

   _____

   _____

   _____

2. Take a few minutes to think about the day in your parenting journey when your child leaves the nest. The door closes behind them and they are on their own. You will still be there when they need you, of course, but now you are in the bleacher seats.

Using the space below or your own notebook, write down the skills and leadership traits you want your child to have when they leave your house. Then jot down any thoughts or ideas you have on adjustments you might need to make to better parent with this end in mind.

Skills and Leadership Traits I Want for My Adult Children	Ideas and Adjustments to Better Accomplish That Goal

Be Grateful for the Grind

When my two oldest granddaughters were born, I promised my daughter we would always take one week a year to host a "grandma" camp, where I watch the kids and mom and dad can have some time off. One of my best friends, Carla, is at a similar stage in life as me. We both have two granddaughters under the age of 5 and she does the same type of thing for her daughter. When we get together, we compare our grandma camp experiences and there is usually much laughter as well as lessons learned in the telling.

One time, before her daughter left, Carla asked for instructions. Her daughter, Mandee, humorously replied, "Keep them alive and don't let Livi torture the cats." Carla and her husband Rick started that grandparent camp with high hopes and full tanks of energy. They were ready to have a fun-filled weekend that would give their daughter and son-in-law a much needed breather. Sounds easy, right? Not really.

Livi was supposed to be taking a nap when Carla heard laughing in her bedroom. As Carla went in to see what was so funny, she discovered that Livi had zipped up one of the cats in a suitcase. The cat wasn't bothered at all, but this certainly fed the grind of the weekend.

You see, this wasn't a simple three hour visit; it was three days. You would think that two adults could handle two girls under five for three days. Theoretically it's easy, but with kids, even the best laid plans can go south in minutes. By the end of the weekend, Rick and Carla were giving into more screen time, more sugar, and fewer naps. And that's after just one weekend!

Parenting doesn't come with just two straightforward instructions: keep them alive and don't let them torture the cats. There are so many facets to parenting. It's as broad as it is deep. It stretches you until you sometimes think you will break. Let me paint a realistic picture for you: you are on a two-decade-plus journey of being worn down while trying to be consistent with your children and balancing your crazy schedule and life. "The grind" is a euphemism to describe the overwhelming stress and exhaustion of everyday parenting. That's the bad news. Yet here's the good news: every day we can choose how we view that grind.

If we focus on the hard parts of the grind, it grows bigger in our mind. We get overwhelmed easily. We give in quickly. We throw up our hands in frustration. If we focus on the beauty of the grind, it grows bigger in our heart. We find patience we didn't have. We stay steady and on mission to find the greatness in our families.

How we manage the mental rollercoaster is what we're going to explore over these next few pages. Grandparents like Carla and I can tap out. Doing life from the bleachers means you can choose when you're going to go out onto the field. The grandparent's time to shine is the halftime show. We are there so our own kids can take a break, then we return to the bleachers and cheer on the family. Even though we come in fresh to the situation, it doesn't take a grandparent long to recognize the familiar, overwhelming responsibility of raising children.

Parents, however, are in the field and focused on the game the whole time. Carla and I know from experience this can be exhausting and when exhaustion builds, even small problems can grow into big ones. Things we value can be forgotten or abandoned in our efforts to just make it through the day with the kids bathed, clothed, and fed. Add in walking the dog, going to work, paying bills, doing laundry, washing dishes, and attempting to hold everything together in one piece and you're sure to get a nomination for being a super-parent.

Parenting can feel like a grind sometimes, but it doesn't have to be a negative one. Once we recognize there's power in the grind that overwhelms us, we can redirect that same power in the grind to motivate us instead. This allows us to be parent overcomers who lead a thriving family!

Recognize the Grind

In our Instagram society, it's easy to want instant gratification from parenting. However, parenting isn't as picture perfect as many of the photos we see, the stories we hear, or the blogs we read. If we don't recognize that parenting is a long process, full of ups and downs, we can catch ourselves thinking, *"How does their family always look so happy in pictures? I must be a terrible parent because I can't even get the kids out the door on time for school without buckets of tears."* That's comparison thinking and it fuels grumpiness in the grind which causes us to feel inadequate as parents. We feel we don't measure up to the awesome-looking parents we see in our social media feed. Negativity is magnified by the comparisons we start making between how we perceive our family to be doing compared to other families. As my friend Jill Savage says in her ***No More Perfect Moms*** book, this happens "when we compare our insides to other people's outsides.[1]"

---

[1] Savage, Jill. *No More Perfect Moms: Learn to Love Your Real Life.* Moody Publishers, 2013. Pg 15.

Of course we contribute to perpetuating comparison thinking ourselves. We tend to want to only post pictures on social media that portray our family as having fun and looking picture-perfect. We like to share the good things that happen with others, but withhold information about the hard stuff.

> *Those other parents are not as perfect as you think they are, and you are a better parent than you give yourself credit for.*

Social media falsely gives the impression that we're peering into the everyday moments of life, but we forget that we can't see what's going on behind the camera, what's been filtered out, or how many pictures it took to get the one that was shared. What we don't realize is that we are often comparing ourselves to a manufactured image of perfection. This is when comparison sneaks into our thinking and sabotages the strength we have as parents. In truth, those other parents are not as perfect as you think they are, and you are a better parent than you give yourself credit for. So viewing the grind negatively is magnified by comparison thinking, but how does it start? Where does this exhaustion of parenting begin? Let's explore that a bit.

As our sweet babies start to grow and develop, they are watching us, trying to mimic our behavior. Adult behavior on a two-year-old doesn't always work well. They can't pour the milk, play outside, or take a walk by themselves. This requires us to slow down our pace and be present with them, tuning into what they need in each stage of life. However, just because our pace is slowed down doesn't mean our mind is. The required slower pace of parenting feels as if it's slowing down our adult lives while at the same time threatening to minimize our dreams.

Especially when our kids are young, we find ourselves managing our everyday life at a rate that seems painfully slow. We can often catch ourselves thinking, "I could do this quicker if someone would just watch the kids." We make "to do" lists in our heads that we worry we'll never accomplish. Meanwhile, our subconscious lists include the "things we're missing out on" and the "things we can't ever get done," creating anxiety. The uneven pace of what our mind is doing and our slowed presence in front of our children creates a grind. Think of two mechanical pieces working together. If one is going fast and the other slow, it is going to get worn down quicker. Frankly so are we. This is why we are often mentally and physically spent at the end of each day of parenting.

In order to move from a gritty, grumpy grind to a grateful grind, we have to deal with our skewed perceptions. Life with kids is slower, messier, and harder than we expect it to be. Parenting is a challenging adventure. Our lives aren't Pinterest perfect, and yes, there is incongruity between the speed of life we're traveling with kids and the speed we want to go. The gritty grind can see that as frustrating, while the grateful grind can see that as enriching. It slows us down enough to smell the flowers, to see a caterpillar through a child's eyes of wonder, or to hear the sensitivities of our child's heart. Of course it's a grind either way, but how we view it can make all the difference in the world.

Choosing to Thrive Above the Grind

Is thriving above the grind possible? Yes, absolutely! However, it requires us to be very intentional about the habits we develop and model for our children.

> One bad moment doesn't make it a bad day. One bad day doesn't make a bad year, and **none of this** makes you a bad parent.

As we dive into some important parenting habits that keep us thriving above the grind, let me assure you that you are the absolute best person to lead your child. You are the one who loves them the most and cares passionately about their present and their future. I'm telling you this because I know from experience that when the grind hits hard, and it will, self-doubt can start sneaking into your thinking. You will have a series of awesome days and you'll feel the joys of parenting, but then a bad day will come along and wreck your intentionality train. When this happens, give yourself some grace, dust off the dirt, and start moving forward again. One bad moment doesn't make it a bad day. One bad day doesn't make a bad year, and none of this makes you a bad parent. You are the best person for the job and are fully able to kick the grind to the curb and thrive in this journey called parenting. So with intentionality in your mind to practice grind-crushing habits and confidence in your heart that you are the best parent for your child, let's dive into these seven habits.

Habit #1: Self-Discipline

My husband wakes up to his alarm clock every morning and walks across the room to turn it off. On top of the alarm is a sticky note with a list of 5 things he wrote down the night before that he chooses to accomplish that day. So instead of turning on snooze and shuffling back into bed, he starts in on tackling his list of priorities. And he doesn't go to bed until all five are finished.

My husband's ability to accomplish to-do lists both baffles and impresses me. His secret is self-discipline.

Now I'm not on my husband's level, but I still use self-discipline. In fact, writing this book has required self-discipline. I don't consider myself a writer. I actually have dyslexia and the thought of writing a whole book intimidated and nearly paralyzed me at first. However, my motive for writing it was important because I want parents everywhere to be inspired and empowered to raise leaders for life. So even though it was hard, I disciplined myself to write, day after day, month after month…because it was important.

What habits and priorities are vitally important to you and your family? The higher your value and motivation, the more likely you are to do those things. Self-discipline is what empowers you to follow through on doing the things that are most important, even on the days when you don't feel like it or when you face one challenge after another.

Habit #2: Rest

If you have been parenting long, you know that when your kids are tired, life is just harder. They're easily irritated, nothing makes sense, and their temper is shorter. The same can be said for you as a parent, too. Everything seems worse when we are tired. So the simple solution would be to get some rest. "But Christina, you don't realize how busy I am! I don't have time to rest!" I definitely know that feeling, so let me share with you some tried-and-true practical strategies for squeezing a little extra rest into your day:

- **Sleep when they sleep**. Go to bed when the children go to bed in the evening or take a nap when your children nap.

I know you have things to do, but you'll accomplish them faster in the morning or after a nap if you're rested.

- **Write down your "to do's."** If you have trouble falling asleep, try making a list to get everything out of your head and onto paper. This way you won't forget the important stuff tomorrow and can safely turn off your brain and fall asleep.

- **Stay off screens one hour before bedtime.** Scientists have actually studied the effects of staring at a screen before going to bed and have found that people can get to sleep much more quickly when they turn off their televisions/phones/computers/etc., a full hour before they want to sleep. The reason, according to Bertrand De Silva, MD, is that, "Night time exposure to blue light—mainly from computers, smartphones, tablets, and e-readers—prevents the release of melatonin, the hormone that tells the body when it should sleep.[2]" So try reading an actual paper book or chatting with your spouse before bedtime and leave the screens turned off.

Being tired is your kryptonite. It will take you down. Rest is a mighty weapon to help you be a super parent.

Habit #3: Consistency

Want secure kids? Be consistent. Seriously, being consistent provides the best form of security for your children. This means your children know that positive behavior is rewarded and that negative behavior comes with consequences. When your

---

[2] https://www.stjhs.org/healthcalling/2017/september/do-you-know-how-screen-time-is-affecting-your-ki/

children know you will not bluff, they'll learn very quickly that the boundaries aren't budging.

Consistency in values is important, too. This means mom and dad have to figure out where they'll land TOGETHER on boundaries and parenting strategies so they can present a united front. Too often one parent is extremely strict and the other parent becomes very lenient, trying to create a perceived balance. This is confusing for kids, though, and can result in them acting differently depending on which parent they are with. Communication is key here. "What did your mom/dad say?" is a phrase that helped my husband and I stay on the same page.

Emotional consistency is also extremely important because our children are watching and learning. If our emotions are out of control, they will learn that emotional rollercoasters are normal and that they can even get extra attention using this. This causes them to subconsciously think, *If Mom and Dad's emotions and temper are not at rest, why should mine be under control?* This is the type of thinking that grows in their mind when we allow our emotions to control us.

Consistency creates a deeply rooted knowledge in your children that they are loved no matter what, that certain things fall outside family guidelines, that you are available, rational, and care deeply about their well-being, growth, and character.

Habit #4: Boundaries

Boundaries also provide security for our kids. When they are clear on boundaries, they know what is acceptable behavior and what is not. If possible, boundaries should to be set proactively rather than reactively. Too often our kids are trying to figure out the boundaries and that's when we react and it feels like we're playing a whack-a-mole game with their behavior. For instance, when you pull into the grocery store parking lot, before you exit the car, let your kids know if you expect them to ride in the cart or walk next to the cart, holding on to it. Let them also know if this is a "you can choose one piece of candy in the check out aisle" trip or a "we're not getting any candy in the check-out aisle" trip.

When we have a standard to stick to, we have something to be consistent with. The boundaries you set will be unique to your family based upon what's important to you. For instance, when setting boundaries around your time, the goal is to have time scheduled into your day to accomplish the most important things. If there are people or activities that might take your family away from the most important things, those people get told no, and those activities get canceled or rescheduled. If friends want to hang out and you tell them no because you have family time scheduled, they'll be okay with that. Or they won't. Either way, you don't have to feel bad for saying no to a good thing so you can spend your time doing a great thing.

> You don't have to feel bad for saying no to a good thing so you can spend your time doing a **great** thing.

We can even teach our children how to respond with a positive no. "No thank you, I don't think that's the best idea," or, "I'm sorry, I won't be able to go this time. My family already has plans," are two examples of positive no's. One thing that helped my children say no, especially in their teen years, was the use of a code word. This was a word or phrase they would

30

use in a sentence when they wanted us to be the bad guy and say "no" for them. Let's say the words were, "chocolate ice cream." If a friend asked them to hang out or go to an event, they would call me and say, "Mom, do we still have the chocolate ice cream in the freezer? Also, so-and-so wants to hang out." I'd know to forbid them to go. Or if they were at a friend's house and felt uncomfortable, they'd call and ask about chocolate ice cream and I would know to immediately go pick them up. It's better to be safe than sorry.

Another area where boundaries are important is helping our children understand the concept of positive and negative peer pressure. Ask your children, "Is this friend having a positive or negative influence on your life?" Having these conversations and helping them navigate how to set boundaries with the people in their life is a gift that will give us peace of mind and keep them safe. It will also help set them up for success in all their relationships.

Screen time would be another area to set boundaries in. When, where, and for how long are TVs, phones, and video games allowed? Are phones allowed at the dinner table? How late is it okay for you to take a work call? How many minutes or hours per day should playing video games be allowed? If you are talking in person with someone, whose texts and calls should be answered immediately and who can be responded to later when you finish your current conversation? The answers to these and other questions will be different for each family. However, setting boundaries that line up with the value you place on quality family time will help your family grow closer and spend more time together.

Habit #5: Pick Your Battles

Picking your battles is an art. When you're living under the same roof with other people and when your kids are always pushing for independence, there will always be battles. The key to thriving above the grind is knowing which ones to ignore and which ones to take on.

In our martial arts academies, there are two battles that we always choose to take on: safety issues and character issues. These must be addressed immediately. Safety issues are pretty easy to identify, but what do we mean by a character issue? An example of a character issue would be lying. The habit of lying will damage their relationships in the future, so it must be addressed now so they can be honest in their relationships as an adult.

The best way we have found to approach these battles in the martial arts school environment is to calmly explain to the student the benefits of changing their behavior. Lay out the consequences, both immediate and long-term, and explain the rewards of changing their behavior. And then, if they don't change, follow through with the consequence. If they do change, they get to experience the rewards.

Some battles may not be worth fighting right now. Like Elsa in Disney's movie *Frozen*, we should remember to sometimes just, "Let it go!" When your child walks out the door with mismatched socks or leaves the toilet seat up, is it worth the excessive drama? Sometimes we just give grace and if we feel it's important to address, we may address it another day when we or they have the emotional energy to handle the correction.

Quick tip: Some children don't respond to an instruction about something not to do until you relate to them how their actions made someone else feel. I experienced this with one of my students. I could say "no" all day long, but until I communicated how his behavior made me feel, the behavior didn't change. This child was so set in his ways, but really had a heart of gold. His behavior changed when he could understand the impact his actions had on others.

Habit #6: Gratitude

If you want to thrive above the grind, this habit is essential. I'll go as far as to say that gratitude completely takes away the power of the grind. It makes parenting worthwhile. It refuels the heart. When we count our blessings, it shows us the beauty of our life.

The absolute opposite of comparison, gratitude shifts us from seeing what's gone wrong to seeing what's gone right. It allows us to see the beauty in each other. When we shift from comparison to gratitude as a parent, we've already won half the battle.

Gratitude allows us to see life through the eyes of a child, catching things we would have missed otherwise. Some days I'm so overwhelmed by my responsibilities that I miss the little moments of joy that are right in front of my eyes. Other days I feel so blessed I want to pinch myself to see if this beautiful life I live is really happening. In the chaos of a busy schedule, or a stressful month, it's easy to miss the little things that bring joy and are gratitude-worthy. It's usually in the quiet moments, often when I'm sitting on my back porch looking at the flowers or watching my fantastic team teach martial arts classes at the taekwondo school, that I realize just how amazing life is.

I encourage you to pause for a moment and really look at your life. Is your family healthy? Be grateful. Do your children laugh often? Be grateful. Is there food in the fridge (even if it's just microwavable meals)? Be grateful. Did you see something beautiful today? Be grateful.

Let an attitude of gratitude permeate your life and I promise you will feel the grind less and less. You won't feel the urge to compare your family or life to others. Your expectations will be realistic. Your contentment will increase. Most importantly, you won't find life lacking because you will realize how rich and full it truly is.

Habit #7: Marriage First

If you're married, you'll be tempted to put all the focus on the kids. It's easy to do because they depend upon you for their very existence. Doing so, though, will increase the grind. You'll feel the tug between the kids and your spouse, increasing conflict and frustration in your marriage.

Your kids, however, need you to prioritize your marriage. Why? There are two primary reasons. First, you and your spouse make up your kids' world. If mom and dad are okay, their world is okay. When you invest in your marriage, you increase your child's sense of security. Of course they won't tell you that, but they will most definitely feel it. Second, you are a role model for your kids and their future marriage. You are setting the foundation for their lifetime perspectives of what a healthy marriage looks like.

Do you have a regular date night with your spouse? It doesn't have to cost a thing…just taking a picnic to the park once a week can do a world of good for a couple to have uninterrupted conversation and focused couple time. The key is putting a regular date on your calendar and keeping it a priority.

Do you and your spouse struggle in marriage? One of the most loving things you can do for your family is to seek help. Set up some counseling appointments, tap into the wisdom of a marriage coach, attend a marriage retreat, and read some great marriage books. If you need a place to start in keeping your marriage a priority or finding healing for a hurting marriage, check out www.NoMorePerfectMarriages.com. It's a great go-to resource for all things marriage.

Welcome to the Real World

Allow me to paint an idyllic picture for you. You have gone through the grind and even risen above it. You've counted your blessings. You've done your best to be disciplined and consistent with your children. You've set boundaries, picked your battles, and tried to incorporate rest into your schedule to create more balance. You've kept your marriage a priority. Now your children have all graduated into adulthood. They fly from the nest like strong, graceful eagles and soar into a successful life in the adult world. They realize now all the sacrifices you made for them as they grew up and shower you with gratitude.

Sounds wonderful, right? Reality check: this isn't always what happens. In fact, I would say it's a rare occurrence.

Sometimes our children stumble into adulthood more like an awkward teenage goose than an eagle. Their coat is half feathers, half down. Their body is all gangly and they look kind of silly as they waddle around next to their peers. And sometimes, we as parents don't hear the gratitude for years to come. In fact, some parents may never receive the gratitude they deserve.

If you are discouraged and feel underappreciated for all your work in the grind of parenting, allow me to share two important words with you: delayed gratification. A thank you could take decades to arrive, and it may never arrive at all. The results of our parenting efforts may take years to appear because our children are still in a growing and maturing process, just like you and me.

So when you are neck deep in the grind, and your children are late for school, and the dog just puked all over the floor, and the dirty laundry looks like the leaning tower of Pisa, remember that this is all temporary. There is still beauty in the middle of the mess. Life is still full of precious moments to be grateful for.

While I would love to give you a cheat sheet on how to be the perfect parent, we both know that's not possible. There are no shortcuts, but there are choices we can make at each fork in the road to be intentional in leading our children. Parenting is unique to every person and every family.

Now that I'm a grandma, let me share a little secret from the far side of parenting. As time passes, you will not even remember the details of the grind. The roughest moments will often fade away. Sometimes they become stories of lessons learned. Like that time your child threw up all over the hotel room in the middle of the night because they ate too much sugar at a buffet the day before? Yup, even that chaotic and terrible moment will be a funny story to share with other parents who have graduated to the bleacher seats. Parenting can be messy even as our kids head into the adult years, but knowing that the daily grind will eventually fade away, helps us to keep that much-needed, delayed gratification perspective.

The Grind Counts

In the karate school we say, "What they see is what they will be." This is a reminder to those who are teaching that we are role models for the kids. In the same way, how we parent in the grind will formulate how our kids learn to handle difficult situations. That's because the grind is really the process of life. We get this amazing training ground with our children to show them how to do life. We model taking chances, handling stress, risking and failing, and risking and succeeding. As they begin stepping out on their own, you will be their safety net for a little while. Expect them to fail…it's honestly how they learn. Then give them unconditional love so they know that nothing they do will jeopardize your love for them.

Eventually you'll work your way to the bleachers knowing you have trained them well. You have walked into battles with them and you have rescued them when it was too much. You were present in the midst of the difficult times and you have rejoiced together when they succeeded. You are a phenomenal parent because of your love for your children. You will have done your best for them.

I hope you're ready to dive into more blessings and challenges of parenting as we continue to walk through these pages together. My prayer is that these words resonate with you deeply and build you up as you continue guiding your children to become confident leaders. You are my hero.

Let's Be Intentional

The 7-7-7 Habit

When my children where little, my husband and I went to a marriage seminar at our church. It was based on a book called *His Needs, Her Needs* by Willard F. Harley Jr, (I highly recommend this book for couples.) One of the most valuable things we received from our weekend marriage retreat was the habit of 7-7-7.

Let me explain how this works. Every seven days (Sundays for my family) we vowed to take the day off, not allowing ourselves to talk business. This was a day for family time, resting and connecting with each other. Everyone looked forward to every Sunday. It was so valuable because at the time we had been using our Sunday down time to catch up and discuss the business, chores, and problems with the kids. The break every seven days protected all of us from the grind of life and allowed space for really connecting on a consistent, weekly basis.

The second seven stands for something my husband and I did every 7 weeks. This is when we would take a weekend to ourselves, with no children. We might have a "staycation" in our own home, or we might stay at a hotel just blocks away. This gave us "grown-up" space to recharge and discuss adult matters, or the needs of the kids, or how we might want to refocus the direction of our family.

The third seven stands for every 7 months when we went on a vacation. Yes, we tried to get away every seven months because we found that our family needed it. When funds were tight, we had to be very creative, but taking time for all of us to rest, play, and enjoy life was a non-negotiable. No matter where we were, the weeks just with our girls were priceless.

We invite you to sit down with your family and get out your calendar and create your own 7-7-7 plan. Set aside sacred time for the family to escape the grind, reconnect, and have fun together.

Avoid Those Dangerous Detours and Distractions

The door flew open to my martial arts school and in tumbled the Clark family. Mrs. Clark had one twin in each hand and their martial arts bags slung over her shoulders. Her face showed her frustration and her body showed her exhaustion. Her oldest son, Alex, was following behind with a smirk on his face; it was obvious he had been up to no good.

I looked at her and asked, "Rough day?" "That's an understatement," she responded. "The kids have been fighting all day. They didn't have school and I had hopes of spending quality family time. Instead, I have been refereeing three fighting kids all day." Alex seemed to have started the trouble and then stepped back to watch the twins fight it out. The twins were too little to understand that their older brother was stirring up trouble.

Anyone who knew Mrs. Clark knew she took great pride in being a good mama. Her kids' hair was always combed. Their clothes were matching and their days were perfectly planned.

"Mrs. Clark, you are looking a little frazzled and stressed; I would love to be a blessing. How can I help you out today?" I asked as I helped the kids get ready to take their martial arts class. After getting them settled in their classes, she and I sat down and chatted a bit. "Are you doing ok?" I asked.

She poured her heart out and explained that her husband had been deployed overseas for three months. He'd already been gone for two months but wouldn't be home for another month. "I'm a terrible mom at the moment. I'm failing my kids. They are growing up hating each other. They are not adjusting well, and honestly I'm not sure what to do."

A random thought came to my mind and I spoke the words almost at the same time I thought them. "Mrs. Clark, I feel like I need to tell you something, and I'm not sure why...You can feed your children cereal tonight."

All of a sudden she burst into tears! "What's wrong?" I asked, worried that I had said something inappropriate. "How did you know?" she asked, crying. "How did I know what?" I responded.

"I always feed them great healthy dinners," she blurted out, "but I was just in the van thinking, *What am I going to make these kids for dinner? I wish I could just feed them cereal tonight.*"

"What's wrong with feeding them cereal this one time?" I said, relieved that my response seemed to be an answer to her unspoken prayer. "How about putting in a movie, eating popcorn, building a blanket tent and having a slumber party in the living room? You would be the coolest Mom. Think about the positive memories you would create!"

"But they have school tomorrow," she said. "I know," I responded, "but it seems that your dream of creating a great family day was stolen from you. We all have lies rolling around in our head trying to steal our joy."

"You're right!" she said, wiping away her tears. I continued encouraging her, "You are a great Mom. I watch you day in and day out love on those kiddos and they know it. And I'm pretty sure they love each other too. One day of feeding them cereal or popcorn won't hurt them, and the memories you create could be just what you need for a happy, healthy family."

"Yes, that's exactly what we are going to do!" she said as she stood to leave. The fresh perspective gave her a new excitement and a dose of hope for a great night of doing nothing but creating memories.

The conversation Mrs. Clark and I had was a conversation that moved her from lies to truth. The lies were screaming at her in the difficult circumstances, but deep down she knew these truths and simply needed to be reminded of them:

- She loves her kids.
- They love each other.
- One day of eating cereal or popcorn won't hurt them.
- She is a great mom.
- She can have fun even on a school night.
- She is stronger than she thinks.
- She will make it through these three months as a single parent.

Once she replaced the lies with positive words of truth, her hope and excitement came back. When I checked back with her a week later, she hugged me and showed me a picture of a blanket tent in the living room with three toothy smiles snuggling around her. Lies are detours and distractions on the journey of parenthood. Mrs. Clark beat those internal lies and you can as well! Once you're winning the war on your own lies, you can help your kids win theirs, too!

Flipping Toxic Self-Talk on Its Head

According to Joyce Meyer, author of the book *Battlefields of the Mind*, every one of us has battles we fight each and every day. These battles take place in our head, often without us even realizing they're there. We have to learn to recognize these wars and win them. Then we have to teach our kids to do the same!

Many of the lies we believe started in childhood when the cement was still wet. In order to identify them, we have to do some remembering. Think with me for a moment: can you recall a time in your childhood when you felt unnoticed, untalented, or unloved? Can you remember when these thoughts got the best of your young mind? As you remember some of those times, let it be a reminder that our children are going through that same internal war.

Just the other day, one of my friend's granddaughters saw a Facebook video of another girl performing a beautiful dance. We all commented on her talent and immediately you could see the self-doubt in my friend's granddaughter rise up as she moped around the house all afternoon. Since a four-year-old can't put her feelings in words, we came to the conclusion that she was feeling jealous of our complimentary words about this other little girl's video. We decided to explain to her that she was a beautiful and gifted dancer, and that God has created many talented dancers to show the world how beautiful dance can be. After that reassurance, she perked right up and went back to being that spunky, soft-hearted little girl.

Lies are brutal no matter what age you are. Lies don't care who you are or even how old you are. They are like a thief trying to steal the good things out of our lives.

Lies steal:

- Our joy.
- Our relationships.
- Our trust in ourselves.
- Our trust in others.
- Our confidence.
- Our hope.
- Our faith.
- Our belief in our abilities.
- Our belief in our futures.

Lies work to give us:

- Fear
- Shame
- Self-Doubt
- Worry
- Depression
- Anxiety
- Insecurity
- Jealousy
- Scarcity
- Loneliness

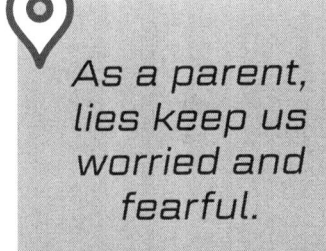

> *As a parent, lies keep us worried and fearful.*
>
> *As a child, lies shape us.*

As a parent, lies keep us worried and fearful. As a child, lies shape us. Personally, I had a lot of anxious thoughts as a child. They seem funny now, but they were very real for me. For instance, I thought that aliens would abduct me or that my father was going to have to protect us from Bigfoot while we were fishing.

After getting lost in a grocery store once, I started having thoughts that my parents were trying to lose me on purpose! No matter how hard my parents tried to assure me that I was loved and wanted, I could not get those thoughts and fears out of my head.

After getting lost, my 5 year-old-self pondered these questions for *years* to come:

- "If this happened once, could it happen again?"
- "If it happens again, what if they can't find me the next time?"
- "Do they *really* want me?"

Even to this day, I partially credit this event for shaping me as a person. I even believe this is one reason why I teach self-defense.

When bad things happen in our lives, we tell ourselves a story about what those events mean about us. When I got lost in the grocery store, the story running through my mind was, "Maybe I'm not wanted." This was not true, of course, but it's so easy for a little lie like that to sneak in and take root in a young mind.

When we tell ourselves a wrong story, we have to learn to write a new story in our mind, a true story that brings us hope and purpose. To illustrate how important it is to recognize the lies and then reframe them with truth, let me share with you Becky's story. Becky was conceived out of wedlock, so her parents had to get married. It was what young couples did at that time.

Her dad always said, "We had to get married and I've had to work three jobs because of you." So whenever her parents fought,

Becky always had an internal reminder that their problems were somehow her fault simply because she had been born. A few years ago, she went on a trip to Washington, DC with a friend. As they stood at the Vietnam Memorial wall, she looked at the dates on the monument of when all these brave soldiers had died. That's when she realized they had all died the year she was born.

A new thought dawned on her and for the first time she saw her life in a different way. Looking at the names etched in marble, she realized that her dad's name could have been on that wall. She looked closer and realized she could see her reflection in the shiny surface. In her mind she thought, *You see yourself right now as the child that caused your parents pain. When you turn around, you are going to realize you are the child that saved their life.*

When she returned home, Becky called her mom, who rarely talked about any facts surrounding her birth. She had to ask, though. "Mom, why didn't Dad go to Vietnam? Was it because he had me to take care of?" "Yes," her mom responded. "You probably kept him alive."

All of a sudden she understood very clearly that if she had not been born, her dad would have likely gone to war and could have died. She realized that being born did not ruin her parent's lives and create a difficult marriage. Her being born quite possibly saved her parent's lives and relationship. That lie she'd told herself her whole life was washed away with this new truth. She could now tell herself a different story. Later that year, she took her dad on a special vacation trip where he opened up and shared that her birth was one of the best events of his life. Wow! The power of truth!

Becky's list of lies looks like this:

- "I was unwanted."
- "I was a burden to my parents."
- "I ruined my parents' lives."

The truth was very different. Here is her new way of looking at her story:

- "I was ~~unwanted~~ wanted."
- "I was a ~~burden~~ blessing to my parents."
- "I ~~ruined~~ saved my parents' lives and relationship."

> **The exact opposite of a lie is where we find the truth.**

The exact opposite of the lie is where we find the truth. Knowing the truth can change our lives. Teaching our children to find the truth can save them years of wrestling with toxic self-talk. You see, the stories we tell ourselves become the messages that shape us. It's the same for our children and that's why our words matter.

Speak Life

If toxic self-talk is an internal battle your child struggles with (and they all do!), would you be willing to take up the sword of Truth-Teller? Would you be willing to help cut away the damaging lies? This means speaking words of life to your child, resisting the temptation to speak words of criticism in frustration. It means looking beneath the surface to identify the lies it seems your child is believing and replacing those with truths about the great gifts and talents you see in them. You may even find it necessary to look for lies that have been a part of your family for years.

Growing up, my dad and I played a lot of football. He taught me so much about the sport, particularly how to throw and catch and clinch it to your chest. I remember one day my dad seemed so proud of my eagerness to learn the sport. I didn't really love the sport so much as I loved making my dad proud. Dad came into the kitchen bragging on me to my Mom. "Mary, you should see Tina catch that ball! She is not afraid of anything. She is going to be a great athlete."

These words stuck with me, and sure enough my Dad was right. I became a great athlete. Or did I? Was I a natural athlete? Or did I merely live up to the words my dad spoke over me?

Personally, I believe the words my dad spoke shaped my life more than my natural abilities. Back then I felt so clumsy and awkward. However, my dad's words and actions helped me to overcome my physical obstacles.

In my childhood, I enjoyed many sports: running track, playing basketball, volleyball, and softball. That's also when I discovered martial arts. I believe these positive sports experiences came about because of my father's continual words of affirmation.

Unfortunately, I have seen the opposite to be true in too many children's lives. When I first started running my own martial arts school, I met with a grandma who was raising her grandson all by herself. I will never forget how she introduced him to me. "Mrs. Newberry, this is my grandson. He is a handful and his father is in jail for stealing and if you don't help him, he will end up in jail too."

I looked down at the defeated little boy and responded with, "I'm sure that's not going to be true. He looks like a good boy to me." The boy smiled at me, but the grandma proceeded to tell me all he did wrong and why she believed he would end up in the same place as his dad.

She kept him in martial arts for awhile. Then she got sick and couldn't bring him any more. Years later, I heard that this little boy did, in fact, end up in jail. My heart broke for him. Inside, I screamed in frustration! He lived up to the words that were spoken over him! There were not enough people in his life telling him that he could end up somewhere different, somewhere so much better.

Our words are powerful. They have the power to build up our children and they have the power to tear them down. My dad spoke words of life to me. That grandma unknowingly spoke words to her grandson that tore him down.

> Our words have the power to build children up...or to tear them down.

It's important for us to not be careless with our words, even in frustration. And if careless words are spoken, it's important for us to apologize and ask for forgiveness. Even in correction you can speak words of life.

For instance, instead of saying, "Here we go again! When are you going to get it right? You never listen to me!" you might say, "I'm disappointed that you didn't listen to me but I know there's a good listener inside of you and that they will show up the next time you need to pay attention to my words." And yes, you may have to say that more than once! Keep calling out who your child has the ability to become!

Generational Lies

As important as it is to speak words of life to your child, it's also very important for you to look at another place lies may be coming from. Extended family and generational communication may be sending the wrong messages, too. Identifying these messages and taking them out of your vocabulary is very important.

Look back at your family's stories. Are there any limiting lies your family believes? Here are some common generational lies:

- "We come from the wrong side of the tracks."
- "We will never be successful or happy."
- "Our family just isn't athletic."
- "We're not intelligent enough to go to college."
- "We've been born with the wrong skin color."
- "Our family has always been poor."
- "All of our family are _____ (you fill in the blank.)"

If you identify some generational lies, it's time for you to draw a line in the sand and determine to move forward differently. Kids often play in the dirt and draw a line and say, "You stay over there. You can't cross this line. That's your side, and this is my side." Drawing a line in the sand as it relates to generational lies means that we are not going to believe these false statements that others may try, unknowingly, to attach to us or our families. We are taking responsibility for restoring the future blessings to our children. This gives them permission to look for the possibilities in life instead of being held back by lies passed on for generations.

When we confront lies, we tackle the trash talk that keeps us or our kids bound up and unable to move forward. It's starts by saying something like this to yourself, "These lies will not continue in my generation or in my lineage! You are not welcome in my head or in my family. Stay on your side of the line!"

> *When we confront lies, we tackle the trash that keeps us or our kids bound up and unable to move forward.*

You see, one side of the line is our past, and the other side is our future. One side believes the lie of defeat, and the other believes the blessing that the best is yet to come. When we look into the future with hope, we have the ability to defeat lies. Standing there waiting for us across the line is the freedom to discover an abundant life, filled with many great treasures yet to be discovered.

What's at stake? Here's what's waiting for your family on the other side of the line: freedom, identity, confidence, peace, excitement, security, contentment, abundance, generosity, community, faith, hope, and love. Certainly you and I long for these things, and so do our children. What's exciting is that we can help them tear down the lies and replace them with truth. We can make a difference!

Start Seeing the Choices

One afternoon my son-in-law pulled me aside and asked me NOT to phrase something a certain way. Let me be honest…at first I was a little offended. However, after I thought about my word choices, I realized he was correct to help me rethink the effect my words had on my grandchildren. Honestly, I'm glad he is taking his role as a father so seriously and monitoring the words that are spoken over his family. I am also grateful that my son-in-law and I have such an honest relationship where he can bring something like this to my attention.

The words we say are powerful. They can bring life or death to a relationship. They can plant lies that limit and shame or they can plant truths that inspire and encourage. The words you and I speak to our children have the power to create passionate, secure, loving adults.

I don't have a lot of regrets in my life. However, I wish I'd had power over my words with my children when I was a younger parent. I didn't realize how my words affected my children when they were little until they were much older and could express how they interpreted those words. As a young mother, I was raising two children and managing two businesses. Sometimes my frustration would spew out of my mouth and float into the atmosphere and land in my girls' thoughts and subconscious. Many times these words were perceived to mean something that was harmful because they were being interpreted by very impressionable children who looked up to me and were sensitive to what I said and how I said it.

Knowing what I know now, I would tell my younger self to choose every word very carefully, because the interpretation of these words will shape and mold my children forever. I would caution myself that every word comes with great responsibility.

A well-spoken word can spark a chain reaction of events that will last for generations. The good news is we get to choose how we use our words. Let's be adults that use our words:

- to inspire and cast vision
- to create possibility thinking and creativity
- to motivate our kids to do their best

- to encourage and call out the strengths of our kids
- to compliment and affirm
- to uplift and speak life
- to praise and see the good
- to connect and see others with eyes of compassion
- to love and listen
- to point out truth and debunk lies
- to correct and point our kids in the right direction

Each and every day you and I get to choose the words we say. Most of the time we don't see it as a choice, but it is. When milk is spilled, we're at a fork in the road. We can fly off the handle in frustration, speaking careless words that plant lies in our child's tender heart, or we can respond with kind grace-filled words that lets them know that everyone makes mistakes. Like best-selling author Dr. Kevin Leman says, "If your child spills milk, he doesn't need a lecture. He needs a rag." Watch for those forks in the road where you have word choices to make.

In the same way that you and I have choices to make, so do our kids. And sometimes they will make poor choices. Your words in those situations will make a difference in how they see themselves and whether they believe their mistakes define them. Oh and by the way, you won't get it right every time. So when you react in anger rather than respond in grace, clean up the relational mess you made. Apologize and ask forgiveness. Be a role model for your kids on how to handle mistakes.

What I want you to remember is that there are no perfect parents. However, let's choose to be intentional imperfect parents who give our children the best tools to make the right choices. At the end of the day, we'll know we did our best and we'll pray like crazy that our kids choose a life full of truth and abundance.

Let's Be Intentional

Grab a pen and paper, sit down in a comfy chair, and spend a few minutes thinking about the answers to these questions:

- What childhood memories have shaped my worldview?
- What childhood memories have shaped my relationship views?
- What was an event in my early life that was negative?
- Is it possible that there are negative thoughts that have led me to believe lies about myself?
- What are those lies?

List three of those lies here in the left hand column:

Lie	Truth

Now that you have your list of lies, go back and draw a line through them. Now on the same line but in the Truth column, insert the opposite—the truth these lies are trying to keep you from believing!

If you need an example to get you started, Becky's list looks like this:

Lie	Truth
I was ~~unwanted~~	I was wanted
I was a ~~burden~~ to my parents	I was a blessing to my parents
I ~~ruined~~ my parents' lives	I saved my parents' lives and relationship

What is the new story you want to tell yourself? What positive messages and outcomes exist in that story? You may have to dig deep to find them. They may take some time to discover, but you are worth the internal journey to find them.

PART TWO

ALL ABOARD

4 Identify Your Location

I remember the day well. Jeff and I learned we would be parents and we were beyond excited. We had scarcely received the report and I was already planning the nursery. Secretly, down deep in my soul, all I could think and pray about was having a baby girl. As the sonogram technician wiped the jelly off my belly, we got the news I was hoping to hear, "You're having a girl!" I felt pure joy wash over me, all the way to my toes! Visions of pink filled my head as I thought about preparing the nursery, filling it with fluffy pink rabbits, big dresses, and even bigger hair bows (after all it was 1989)!

Melanie Marie was born July 16, 1989, with a head full of dark hair and china doll eyes. I dreamt of our idyllic future with our daughter while I was recovering in the hospital. Reality hit hard when Jeff brought Melanie and me home. I quickly realized that parenting, in addition to being a beautiful blessing, was an intense, 24/7 job filled with sleepless nights and exploding diapers.

Jeff and I were no longer those two naive newlyweds. We were stressed with all our responsibilities. Overwhelmed with parenting, we put our marriage on the backburner. Business at our fledgling martial arts school was picking up during this time. Trying to be a mom, a wife, and a business owner all at the same time felt like juggling seven balls while riding a unicycle across a tightrope. *This wasn't the stuff of my dreams. Why was being a parent so hard?* I was in desperate need of some direction. Luckily for me, God sent the right person along at the right time to mentor me and help restore equilibrium to my life.

Intervention

The year Melanie was born, I met the Brown family. They came into our academy and, thankfully, into my life. They didn't have much as far as material possessions; however, they did have a ton of love between them. Kathy, the mom, sacrificed to keep her kids in our program. I was amazed at how confident, smart, and joyful the kids were, despite their family having some obvious challenges. You see, Kathy was a single parent. She had one child with learning disabilities and the other on the autism spectrum. She seemed like a super mom to me, juggling her responsibilities at work and home like a pro, remaining calm in situations that would flabbergast me. How did she do it?

One day I felt comfortable enough in our relationship to ask her about it. "Kathy, what is your secret? I know you are facing some uphill challenges, and yet, your family always seems so happy and so confident. And you always seem so calm." I didn't come out and say it, but she intuitively understood that I was worried I wouldn't be good at this parenting thing. I was more than just curious. I was self-doubting, overwhelmed, and fighting anxiety at the time.

She smiled and without hesitation answered, "Parenting is all about balance." Something clicked in my brain and all of a sudden I knew why my life felt like a bizarre circus act: because being a parent required balance and I was untrained in this area. "Wow. That sounds so simple. But I still have no clue where to start," I responded.

"Let me explain," Kathy said, and that conversation sparked the beginning of a mentorship that changed my life. Over the years of our friendship, Kathy worked with me through several different areas of my life where balance needed to be restored. She helped me figure out exactly where I was as a parent and where I wanted to be. Then Kathy walked with me and helped me change and grow. I would be honored if you would allow me to share Kathy's words of wisdom along with some of my own so you can know where you are in relationship to where you need to be.

Where Are You on the Map?

I live in the flatlands of Illinois, surrounded by cornfields. Every day I make the 15 minute drive from a rural town to the bustling city of Champaign-Urbana. As the year passes, I get to watch the cycle of farming during my commute to work. In the spring, the farmers are out plowing their fields into straight lines of dark, freshly turned over earth. Over the summer I watch the corn go from light green specks in the ground to towering stalks of dark green with yellow tassels. In the fall they fade to a warm tan before the farmers gather it all up into their grain silos. The fields then lie empty and desolate all winter and the whole cycle starts over in the new year. I enjoy watching the process every time.

Think about those vast cornfields with me for a moment. Now imagine if someone picked you up and dropped you in a sea of cornfields, and then spun you around seven times so you no longer knew which way was north, south, east, or west. And then they asked you to walk to Chicago. Would you be able to get there? I certainly wouldn't. What would you ask for first? Probably a map. But even having the map is useless if you don't know where on the map you currently are! If you don't know where you are, how can you ever be expected to figure out where you need to go?

When I was a young parent, I realized pretty quickly that I needed a map. It took a little longer and a lot of help for me to realize that I also needed a reality check regarding where I was on the map. For a time, as a young parent, I was stuck in the middle of the cornfield with no sense of direction. Then I'd find my way only to discover a new season of parenting when I'd feel lost again. It was my mentors who pointed me in the right direction many times to navigate the ups and downs of parenting.

Now I have three beautiful, successful, grown up daughters who are kicking butt (we are a taekwondo family after all) and taking names in their corner of the world. I also have dozens of honorary children who, although they don't call me "mom", still look to me as a guiding voice in their lives. If you will allow me, I want to walk you out of the cornfield. And I believe deep in my heart that you have every ability to change and create more of the balance your heart so desperately needs. So let's dive in! Let's take a look at the different areas of our lives, identify where we are, and consider the areas where balance needs to be restored.

ONE: Balance Love and Discipline

Here's a small peek into the reality of my world: most families bring their children into my martial arts academy for one of two reasons: a lack of confidence or a lack of discipline. I can always tell from their first private class, called an orientation, which it is. Sometimes the kids are bouncing off the walls and the parents are looking at me in desperation, wanting me to give their child some kind of structure and discipline. When their child is blatantly disrespectful, the parents gently try to coax their children to cooperate. Other times the child is painfully shy, unwilling to come out from underneath their parent's chair. Even after I get them out and start a mini taekwondo class, they constantly look to mom and dad for approval, worried that their actions might somehow be disappointing to their parents. Too often when I attempt to teach this fearful child some moves and they make a small mistake, the parents correct them from the sidelines.

That first lesson begins a relationship of teamwork and trust between the parent and the instructor working together to help the child grow into a leader, gaining confidence or discipline and sometimes both. If the parents are open to it, we have real conversations with them about the patterns we see in their child's life and what we perceive to be the cause of it. We teach the children balance in their martial arts classes and help the parents gain balance in their families.

In my experience, I've found that when there is an abundance of rules and controlling behavior from parents, the result is an increase in the child's likelihood to be resentful and turn to rebelling against authority. I'm no scientist or psychologist, but I do know that for every action there is an equal and opposite reaction. Kids that live under their parents thumb often react in the worst possible ways. Sometimes it happens while they are young. Other times they silently comply and then go haywire when they move off to college and experience a taste of freedom for the first time. Rebellion can also happen when children are given no discipline because they grow up without respect for their parents or any authority.

> *Children thrive best in a balance of equal parts love with equal parts discipline.*

Of course we can't just let our kids run wild and we also can't rule them with an iron grip of control. My mentor Kathy told me that children thrive best in a balance of "equal parts love with equal parts discipline."

When you really think about it and boil down why rules are in place and enforced it is because of both love and relationship. When we take the time to explain this to our children, they get to see first-hand why rules exist. It's even better still to give them input on the house rules. This empowers them to be fully committed to the family and remain respectful of the boundaries. It also reduces your need to say, "Because I told you so!"

How can we balance love and discipline in our families? We begin by examining the "why" behind the rules in your house. Be ruthlessly honest: are your rules set in place for safety and love or for convenience and control? Discuss rules in place for safety and love with your kids. Allow them to talk about the guidelines and give input in an effort to better understand them. Also, don't be afraid to hold them accountable to the rules the family has agreed upon. Finding the balance between love and discipline is what intentional parenting is all about.

TWO: Balance Education and Wisdom

Did you know that in some countries parents will have their children work with tutors before school, then they attend a full school day, and then visit additional tutors after school? This was so prevalent in one country that the government had to step in and regulate how much educational time a child could endure in one day.

Even here in the U.S. I've seen similar educational pressure put on children. However, I started noticing a pattern that these same children with fantastic test scores tend not to make any decisions for themselves. Many times I have been teaching a martial arts class and see a child who is too close the cubbies at the edge of the training mat, where it was unsafe for them to be kicking and practicing. They would not take the initiative to move out of the way unless they were told repeatedly. Their intellect was off the charts, but their common sense was alarmingly absent.

When we teach our children to use common sense, we start by giving them an education and then help them apply that learning in real life. We call this wisdom. For example, a child may know the definition of a hematoma (education), but do they know how to prevent one (wisdom)?

I've already shared some of the things I did wrong as a parent. Here is one thing we did right: we complimented our girls for having good grades, praised them for demonstrating wisdom, and rewarded them when they began a self-initiated pursuit of something they were passionate about. This was how they developed a life-long love of learning.

When our daughters got in trouble, they were grounded until they finished reading a chapter in a fabulous but now out-of-print book called *The Wisdom Book*. The chapter they read would directly relate to their violation. They also had to write a report on it. In this way, grounding was linked to growing, not punishment.

Education is incredibly important. Knowledge and education are catalysts for innovation. Education helps us find solutions to the world's toughest challenges. It's leaders who are able to take that education and wisely apply it in their everyday life so that everyone can benefit from it.

Author and speaker Craig Groeschel said in one of his popular podcasts, "When you delegate tasks you create followers. When you delegate authority, you create leaders." We help our children grow in wisdom when we give them some authority in their own lives. Yes, that means they have to be given the freedom to fail and make mistakes. However, it also means they have the opportunity to learn how to think for themselves. That's the heart of wisdom and being able to discern that you're too close to the cubbies to practice your kicks!

How do we balance education and wisdom for our children? Intentional parents prepare their children in both of these areas. That means valuing and encouraging your children in their educational pursuits. It also means we don't tell them everything they need to do, encouraging them to think for themselves. Finally, it means being actively involved in teaching them how to use their education in practical ways.

THREE: Balance Enabling and Empowering

It was a Tuesday evening and the kids were rocking it in class. Not only that, but we were staying on track with my class planner, which is rare. Then it happened. Someone's belt fell off.

In that moment when the belt hit the floor I was at an immediate crossroads: I could direct an assistant to go over and retie it, or I could use this incident as a teaching moment. I chose the teaching moment. "Alright everyone, let's learn how to tie our own belts!"

It took ten whole minutes and the help of the black belts that I dragged over from the other side of the mat to watch and help the kids practice. But by the end of those ten minutes, every single kid, five-years-old and up, could tie their belt correctly all by themselves. I could tell from looking at the parents faces that some of them were annoyed at us using ten minutes of valuable class time for a belt tying lesson when it would have taken ten seconds to retie the one belt. However, most of them were white belt parents who hadn't been in my academy quite long enough to know what this training was really about.

I decided to clue them in, "Parents, give these kids a big hand! They can now tie their own belts all by themselves and you don't have to do it anymore. I'm so proud of their leadership and independence!" I went on to give the students a brief pep talk about how their job was to grow in independence so they could be successful leaders as adults. "Should your parents carry your gear bag?" "NO!" "Do your parents have to tie your uniform and belt on?" "NO!" "Do they have to get everything ready for you to go to taekwondo class?" "NO!" "Who can do those things from now on?" "ME MA'AM!" By this point all of the parents were nodding their heads in a silent, "Amen!"

My job and passion is to help kids grow up into leaders. I can't do that if I always tie on their belts for them. Neither can you.

Because parents have been around the block a few times, they are much faster at tying shoes, packing lunches, carrying backpacks, understanding homework, and cutting waffles into bite sized pieces. But just because we CAN do things faster doesn't mean we SHOULD. When our kids are little, we do a lot for them. The problem is we can forget that as they grow up, their level of independence should increase. Parents should grow too; grow themselves right out of a job!

> *When we do something for our kids that they can do for themselves, that's enabling.*
>
> *When we teach them how to do something so they can do it themselves, that's empowering.*

When we do something for them they can do for themselves, that's enabling. When we teach them how to do something so they can do it themselves, that's empowering. Had I asked an assistant to tie on the little guy's belt, it would have enabled him. By stopping and teaching, I moved into empowering. Did it take time? Yes. Will it save time in the long run? Absolutely.

A word of warning: resist, Resist, RESIST! Your kids will try to sweet talk you into doing things for them that they should be doing on their own! My own daughters perfected the puppy dog eyes and let me tell you, they are sometimes hard to say no to. But I know that insisting they do something on their own is setting them up for success in the future. However, children don't learn by osmosis. We have to slow down and take the time to teach them. I can't demand a student tie his or her own belt unless I've first taught them how and assisted them once or twice.

How can your family balance enabling and empowering? The best way to start is by allowing them to make mistakes and even celebrating those mistakes. I care about this so strongly that I'm devoting a whole chapter to it a little later on. Brainstorm with your child and come up with a few tasks they want to learn to do by themselves. Then take the time to teach them how, assist them as the practice, and then watch and cheer them on as they do it all by themselves!

FOUR: Balancing Correction and Compliments

Every instructor I've ever trained naturally leans in one direction or the other. Some have a natural bent towards encouraging students with compliments. They see all the good in the students and rarely, if ever, confront the bad. Others have eyes that can pick out what each student needs to work on and they aren't afraid to approach the student about their shortcomings. As you read this, you have probably already decided in your own mind which you think is better. But here's the thing, every good martial arts class has instructors who know how to use both approaches in their teaching. Every successful family also has parents that utilize both approaches as well.

Children that only hear correction soon feel they are never enough. Their efforts are wasted because no one notices their progress. This mental discouragement can happen even when the corrections are only being made because the parents see so much potential and their heart's truest intention is to help their child grow.

On the other hand, children that only receive compliments and are never confronted about bad behavior or bad habits will develop a false sense of self. This false sense is dangerous! When they grow up they will be rudely awakened to the fact that the world is not as easily impressed as their parents were.

How can your family balance correction and compliments? Find what your natural bent is and takes steps to practice the opposite skill. It's also worth noting here that one parent doing all of the correcting and the other doing all of the complimenting is NOT balance in this area. When both parents work together as a team and move towards the middle ground, there is consistency for the children, not contradiction. This gives them security and peace of mind, no matter which parent they are with. I'd like to give a huge shout out to all the split household families I've had the privilege of knowing at the academy who work through their differences and give their child consistency no matter which house they are in.

FIVE: Balance Work and Play

Do you know that children learn best through play? While teaching them to have a diligent work ethic is important, play is also incredibly valuable. This was a lesson I learned late in the game, however. My oldest still bears scars from the workaholic season of my life. Through most of her childhood, I valued work very highly and saw little need for play. I eventually learned that children and adults can't thrive unless there is some enjoyment and play in their lives. Now that we're both adults, we are both beginning to learn how to relax and play. We've begun to actively explore enjoyable activities that we can use to restore play and a bit of balance to our busy lives.

Please learn from my mistakes! Play is what brings out the joy in life. It's a shame to see those we love work an entire career in a job they hate only to retire and realize that their body and their circumstances don't allow them to do the things they'd always dreamed of together. I'm now choosing to find ways to enjoy my life right now, while still getting work done. If you tend to be a Type A, driven personality where work is king, I want to encourage you to do so, too.

I've also seen the opposite extreme take place: families that value activities and toys so much that a pursuit of play takes over their lifestyle at the cost of habits of responsibility. Repairs on the home fall by the wayside and financial responsibilities get neglected. This can create an atmosphere of unreliability, and the children grow up with the scars of uncertainty and lack the disciplined habits of success. There's definitely a balance to be found in work and play.

In the book of Ecclesiastes in the Bible it says that, "There is nothing better for a person than that he should eat and drink and find enjoyment in his toil." If all we do is work and we never pause to rest, to refresh ourselves or enjoy the fruits of our labor, we are missing out on living. On the other hand, we can't avoid the responsibilities of life.

Work comes before play, but play ought to come after work. I also happen to firmly believe that work doesn't have to be hard. With the right attitude and the right people, work can be play. When my co-writer Olivia was growing up, every time her family cleaned house for the holidays, they started by plugging a Mannheim Steamroller Christmas Album into the CD player. Then their whole family of seven jammed out as they picked up, vacuumed, and dusted. It was a team effort done to the impressive soundtrack that still signifies the holiday season in many of their minds today.

How can your family balance work and play? Find ways to accomplish work as a team and experiment to see what makes the work more fun. Determine what kinds of fun activities each family member would like to do afterwards and set that as a reward to keep people motivated. Also, find your jam and play it loudly. Mannheim Steamroller doesn't have to be your music. It can be Audible books, or your favorite movie soundtrack. The most important thing is that you're enjoying work and planning for play!

Change Your Hat

I wouldn't be a good guide to you if all I do is talk about balancing your children's lives and never mention balance in your own life. Let's think of this from a hat perspective. I wear a lot of different hats. Not actual hats, but metaphorical hats. I have my wife hat when I'm spending time with my husband and investing in my marriage. When I'm getting my nails done with my daughter, I'm wearing the mom hat. When I'm growing my martial arts academy or teaching my students, I'm wearing the business owner or teacher hat. Of course there's also the daughter hat, the grandma hat, and the mentor hat.

All of this hat business can get confusing! The problem comes in when I put a hat on and forget to take it off. For example, my daughters don't always want the mentor hat on. Sometimes they just need me to be mom and be quiet and empathetic as I simply listen to them. I also can't send my wife hat away on vacation because I'm so busy with my business and mom hats. That doesn't work well either.

Honoring yourself in the process of parenting means remembering that our lives are multi-faceted. Parenting is a huge part of our lives, but it is only a part. There are other parts of your life that need attended to if you want to stay in balance. Wear that parenting hat with pride, but remember to change into your other hats because they are an important part of YOU as well. When your kids graduate and move out of the house, your mom or dad hat will probably sit on the shelf a lot more often than it used to. When that happens, make sure you still know how to rock those other hats!

Let's Be Intentional

Is your family in balance? Take just a few minutes to assess yourself, your family, and your parenting style. I recommend that you find a quiet space to evaluate and really think through this.

Let's imagine you are going to walk across a tightrope. (Or, more realistically, ride across it on a unicycle.) If you lean too far to one side or the other, you're going to take a tumble.

Below you'll find the 5 areas of balance we've talked about in this chapter. Rate yourself on a scale of 1 to 5 in each area. A 3 means you feel your family has achieved perfect balance, while a 2 and 1, 4 and 5 all indicate varying degrees of imbalance, of leaning more towards one extreme or the other.

Work				Play
1	2	3	4	5
Correction				Compliments
1	2	3	4	5
Empowering				Enabling
1	2	3	4	5
Love				Discipline
1	2	3	4	5
Education				Wisdom
1	2	3	4	5

My hope is that as you read the remaining pages of this book, you will restore your family to a life of abundance and balance. We can start that restoration process right now. In the space provided on the next page or in a separate notebook, choose 3 areas we've talked about in this chapter and write down one change you would like to implement that will help create the balance that will allow your family to thrive and grow together.

1. Area: _____

   Change: _____

   _____

   _____

   _____

   _____

2. Area: _____

   Change: _____

   _____

   _____

   _____

   _____

3. Area: _____

   Change: _____

   _____

   _____

   _____

   _____

5 Choose Your Traveling Companions

When I first met Jason and Katie, our relationship was a business one. They are photographers who visit martial arts schools across the country and take fantastic pictures of the students. I've had a lot of photographers visit my school over the years and Jason and Katie are simply the best. As I got to know them, though, I soon began to admire not just their talent and professionalism, but also their passion and character. It was only a matter of time before our business relationship turned into a friendship.

One day I mentioned that I enjoy walking and would love to go hiking someday but didn't know the first thing about how to get started. They were avid hikers and suggested they take me on my first big girl hiking trip. I was ecstatic. You see, I certainly could have asked a lot of people to go with me on this hiking journey. There were others who could have helped me figure it out, but I really wanted to hike with Jason and Katie for two primary reasons.

First, I enjoy being around them. Their conversations always inspire me, and there is never any drama with them. We share similar passions, interests, and convictions. I wanted to do life with them and hiking seemed like a good way to build that relationship. The second reason was that I knew they understood all the ins and outs of hiking. They knew where to go, what to bring, what kind of shoes to wear, how to pack your backpack, and more. If anyone could show me the ropes and keep me safe in the wilderness, it was them.

Parenting requires the same kind of intentionality when it comes to choosing our traveling companions. As parents, we need to consider the kind of people with whom we want to surround ourselves. Who do we want to bring with us in our parenting journey? We want to find people we enjoy, who are going in the same direction as us, who maybe have more experience and resources than us, and those who are willing to walk with us along the path of parenting. If you are hiking, find a good hiker to go with you. If you are a parent, the same principle applies. You need to find some other good parents to hang with. When I was a young parent, I realized quickly that I had no clue where I was going. Remember Kathy? She was my parenting guide, much like how Jason and Katie became my hiking guides.

The destination Jason and Katie picked for my first hike was Zion National Park in Utah. The trip was a team effort. The park doesn't want the trails to get overcrowded and overused, so you have apply months in advance to get permission to hike them. Jason and Katie applied for the permit and I booked the hotel room.

The day started perfectly. The weather was gorgeous, not too hot, not too cold. Before we hit the trail, Jason checked our backpacks, making sure they fit right and were filled with the right amount of water and snacks for the journey. He looked at everything carefully because he wanted us all to be safe and successful.

Zion is one of the most beautiful places I've ever been. The colors are beautiful. There are dozens of shades of green, pools of teal water, and gorgeous orange canyon walls. At one point I stumbled into a bush that I didn't realize was alive. Hundreds of brightly colored butterflies fluttered up around me when I bumped into their home. What a magical experience!

The trail we were hiking is called the Subway Trail. It's a slot canyon, carved out by water. At one point in the trail you can actually see dinosaur tracks! As a kid I always wanted to see dinosaur tracks; now my childhood dream was going to become a reality.

We climbed straight down the canyon into the creek bed that had been carved out by water for thousands of years. Once you're in the canyon you can't hear cars, or anything industrial or man-made. There aren't even any other people. There's just you, your companions, and the quiet stillness of nature. When we arrived at that spot on the map where the tracks were supposed to be, we started looking. We looked on the path, in the woods, and in the creek bed. No dinosaur tracks. Jason, who knew just how much I wanted to see the tracks, said, "You ladies wait here and rest. I'll go look around a little more."

In the same way that Jason took over in the hunt for dinosaur tracks, we need other parents to do the same for us on our parenting hike. When choosing people to walk with you on your parenting journey, it's wonderful to find someone who will let you rest for a little bit while they do some heavy lifting. These are people who truly have your family's best interests at heart. They are the friends you need in your parenting community!

As Katie and I sat on a rock and caught our breath, we could hear Jason. He was in the woods, up and down the mountain, around the mountain, all over the place looking for those silly tracks. I leaned back and put my hand against the rock to rest and study the map. I felt a weird indentation in the stone and got up to see. Wouldn't you know it, we had been sitting right on top of the dinosaur tracks the whole time!

From the level of excitement, I probably looked like a 5-year-old getting a puppy for Christmas. We cheered and yelled for Jason, but he couldn't hear us. He was still too far away. He was so dedicated to finding those tracks for me, and I believe this determined part of his character is one of the reasons I admire him so much.

Katie and I put our hands in the footprints and traced the tracks up the rock, taking pictures and videos. I have a video from that day and I still watch it every once in awhile, remembering that great moment when we realized we had been sitting on the dinosaur tracks all along. But it's not just the dinosaur tracks that I enjoyed. I loved this trip because I got to spend time with two dear friends. Jason and Katie are busy people and could have been doing a million different things. Instead they were sharing their hiking experience with me. That day is now a precious memory of time spent in beautiful Zion with my special friends.

I have similar memories with those whom I have traveled the journey of life. We're not designed to do life alone and neither are our kids. Our kids need certain people, voices, and messages along their hike in life. Let's take a look at some of these valuable relationships.

Mentors

My daughters are all grown up now with my youngest just turning 18 a few days ago. They are strong, independent young women who still call us for advice sometimes. This makes my husband and I happy. They don't need us like they used to, but they still allow us to be a voice of wisdom and influence in their lives. That's a huge honor we don't take lightly.

However, when they were growing up, it wasn't always our voices they listened to. It was Mr. Fink's voice that held all the sway. Mr. Fink was their high school science teacher and I'm pretty sure my girls thought he walked on water. I can't count the number of times my girls came home from school and said, "Mom, Dad, Mr. Fink said…". And it turns out he said the exact same thing we'd been telling our daughters for months! We were thinking, "What the heck?! Why didn't they hear it from us?!"

My husband was very wise, though. He didn't allow his ego as a parent to get in the way of his daughters' personal growth. So at the next parent-teacher meeting, he pulled Mr. Fink aside and asked if he could maybe mention a few things to our daughters that we wanted them to learn as life lessons. "Of course!" he responded. Mr. Fink was perfectly willing to be another voice in our children's lives. We could have been frustrated by the fact that our children listened more to their favorite teacher than to their own parents, but instead, we were glad they were learning. It doesn't matter as much where they heard it as long as they heard it and grew into better leaders because of it.

Yes, your children desperately need to hear your voice and your wisdom. And yes, sometimes they won't listen to what you say, so it helps to have secondary role models in your corner. These mentors can come in many forms. It could be an aunt or an uncle, a grandparent, a coach, a school teacher, or a martial arts instructor. These positive voices of influence will help plant seeds of wisdom in your child that will allow for a full harvest in those teen and adult years. It's also incredibly helpful to keep doors of communication open for others to speak into their lives. This allows your children a safe place to go when they don't see eye to eye with you, which happens a lot when they become teenagers!

Your children will benefit greatly from positive role models, but not all adults in their lives are a positive influence. We don't ever want our children to be led in the wrong direction, so we have to be good judges of character when deciding who we allow to speak into our children's lives. What should we look for in a mentor for our families? There are two characteristics we want to see.

Character

The best mentors for our children walk the walk. We learned early on in our career that picking instructors who were excellent martial artists and might have been really pleasant to look at, came with a price if they didn't have phenomenal character. I can teach anyone how to punch and kick, how to teach, how to follow systems; that's all easy. However, character is far more important and much harder to teach. I would rather hire someone with phenomenal character and crappy kicks because I can teach kicks much easier than character.

To live day in and day out always wondering if the people on your team are going to represent you well is both mentally and emotionally exhausting. However, I go to character examining extremes when hiring a role model for students that aren't even my own children. When we can, we should also go to great lengths to examine the character of the adults who are influencing our children's lives.

So what do we look for? The marks of a role model with character include being fiercely loyal to their own family and spouse, having discipline in their own life, and being well respected in the community. The best mentors use their words wisely, not gossiping or arguing, but speaking with wisdom and encouragement. Another sign of good character is generosity in giving grace to you, your child, and themselves. We are all bound to make mistakes as we grow. When that happens, mentors with character are quick to forgive and believe in giving second chances. Most of all, you will know you have found a person of character when their walk matches their talk. In other words, they have integrity. They are already producing in their own life what you want them to help you produce in your child's life.

Mentors can be a huge benefit, and they can also be very disastrous to our children without proper checks and balances. People who are sexually assaulted usually know their attacker personally. While we highly advocate that our children have mentors, these mentors should have very strong boundaries of their own. We as parents must keep our eyes open and set up healthy boundaries around our children. In fact, if potential mentors don't have time, place, and conversational topic boundaries of their own, this is a HUGE red flag.

Character counts in every mentor. We have the responsibility of being very aware of who has access to our families and our children. Intentionally placing people of character in our children's lives is one of the best gifts we can give them.

Committed

Strong mentors in our children's lives are people who are willing to walk the extra mile. When martial arts instructors get together, they often share stories about their students. One of my all time favorites comes from Mr. Gilbert, who is a force of positive energy wherever he goes. He encouraged his students to clean their rooms and threatened to make house calls to check if they didn't do it. Little Charlie did not clean up like he was supposed to and his parents told Mr. Gilbert. Later in the week Mr. Gilbert stopped by the house. Charlie answered the door and froze in terror, jaw hanging down by his knees. Then he slammed the door and ran to his room and began rapidly throwing toys and dirty clothes and trash around, suddenly desperate to clean. His mom re-opened the front door in confusion to see who it was that had caused her son's strange behavior. Her confusion was cleared up when she saw Mr. Gilbert standing out there with a huge grin on his face.

The best mentors are committed to doing whatever it takes to help your child grow. Mr. Gilbert, who had over a hundred students at the time, was that parent's hero because he was willing to take the time out of his busy workweek to make a personal visit to increase the leadership and discipline of one student. You have found a phenomenal mentor when you find someone who is willing to go far out of their way to help your child succeed.

Mentors are also committed to doing life with your family. They are in it for the long haul, through all the ups and downs of life. We don't disown our family members when they make mistakes or abandon them in their time of need. The same is true of a good mentor. When life gets tough, our true community of mentors and coaches get tougher. The problem with this is that sometimes you must go through hard situations in order to see who is truly committed, who truly is WITH you on this parenting journey.

Finding deeply committed people means being truly committed ourselves. It means we serve, lead, and love the people we have chosen to do life with. Your family's mentors may mess up, but they'll never give up. You or your child may mess up, but they'll never give up on your family.

Mark Ambrose says, "Show me your friends and I'll show you your future." The people we surround ourself with will determine the direction our life is headed. I would take it a step further than Ambrose. Show me the adults whose voices most strongly influence your child, and that will be your child's future.

Guiding Friendships

Looking backward in this parenting gig, I now see that every friendship my children had when they were young proved to be crucial for their adult life. When they were young, I chose friends for them that I knew would be positive influences. When they grew older, I had to let go of the reins a little and allow them to choose their own friends. Wow was that hard! But the things they learned while they navigated these friendships showed them what they did and didn't want in a friend or spouse. I couldn't be more proud of their relationship choices as adults. I'm pretty sure I have the best son-in-laws in the world (and I'm also sure I'm completely biased)!

The truth is, when our children start growing up, they begin to gather friends who we may or may not be fond of. There will even be times when our children will actually prefer their friends over us. Talk about painful! Intentional parenting means that even though they may not come to you nearly as often for advice on friends, you are always within arms reach. They know you are ready to be a listening ear and a voice of wisdom.

When we teach our children what to look for in a friend when they are young, doors will be opened for us to continue the conversation when they are entering those treacherous teen years. Some children may be more introverted and less prone to go out and make friends. Others may be so outgoing and talkative, but they struggle with forming deep friendships. Equipping your child with the tools to make good friends and be a good friend is a priceless gift you can give him or her. Intentional parents equip their children with the tools to reach out to others. Here are some of the tools I found most valuable to teach.

Smile

On one occasion, Olivia's mom asked me why we hired her. I said, "Because she smiles all the time." That was the simple answer. Her smile made people feel comfortable and welcome, so my husband and I hired her to work at the front counter and welcome people into the school. That's how she started, and that opened the door for us to become such great friends. Without that great smile of hers, this relationship might not have formed and this book might never have been written.

People treat you differently when you smile. A warm, genuine smile can break down barriers of hostility and open up doors of opportunity. Actually having your child practice looking people in the eye and smiling at them can have a huge impact on the way their peers perceive them at school. It also gives them endless opportunities to brighten other people's day, because when we smile at others, they almost always automatically smile back.

Make Introductions

It was Will Rogers who said, "You never get a second chance to make a first impression." He's absolutely right. You create a first impression within the first 30 seconds of greeting someone. Introducing ourselves with confidence is not a matter of personality but rather of practice. We can help our children learn how to confidently introduce themselves by practicing until it becomes natural. Here is a great way to practice with your child:

CHILD: Hi, my name is _____. What's your name?

PARENT: I'm _____.

CHILD: It's nice to meet you, _____."

Once they are comfortable practicing with you, have them do it with siblings, with relatives, and then encourage them to try it out on the playground or at school. If you are not sold on the idea of scripted practice yet, just imagine your child being the leader in their class, going up to every child and having the confidence to introduce themselves.

Carry on a Conversation

Talking doesn't make good friends. Asking the right questions and really listening does. Have you ever watched some of the great leaders of our time? You might notice their ability to carry a conversation, build rapport, and listen with a sincere interest to understand the other person's perspective and emotions.

My friends at Klemmer and Associates, a leadership development and training company, call this "be with" listening. Really being present. Phone away, eyes engaged and asking questions to understand and deepen the relationship. Just think of all the years your family has in front of you to practice "be with" listening. In this cell phone world, it's a great practice for all of us to intentionally be with our children, giving their hearts what they deeply desire: our undivided attention. It's also a great way to teach them to be good listeners.

I invite you to play a game that will help your child develop the ability to carry on a conversation. Sit across from each other with a ball and start a conversation by asking a question. The asker then tosses the ball to the other person. They can not pass the ball until they answer and then ask a question to the other person. The object of the game is to move the ball as many times as possible. This little drill will help your child practice asking questions and listening, both vital for carrying on a conversation. Asking deeper questions and follow up questions will help them show a sincere interest in the other person.

Compliment

As our children grow up, they will eventually find that not everyone wants to be their friend. They'll also discover not everyone is a good friend. Inevitably, they will meet someone who has not been taught how to be kind with their words, and hurtful and critical words will fall upon their ears. We can't protect them from all the negative words out there. We can, however, equip them to respond with confidence and grace, so that the criticisms have little influence over their mood or sense of worth.

One of our secret weapons in the academy to help kids in a bullying situation is something we call, "Compliments Crush Criticism." When someone criticizes your child or calls them a name, they can respond by giving the other person a genuine compliment. The unsuspecting bully will be surprised and disappointed because the response is not what they expected. They may also be uplifted by your child's positive words. Here's how to practice:

Call your child a name. Please don't use an actual mean name. When my students practice at the martial arts academy, we have them call each other "purple" as a pretend mean name.

PARENT: "You're purple!"

CHILD: "I like your _____!"
(be sure to have them practice saying it with a smile.)

Then your child turns and walks away cheerfully.

Practice this over and over until your child's first reaction is to find something nice to say about the other person. What happens over time is that their minds become trained to compliment before they criticize. Bullies have a hard time continuing their rants when they are being complimented. It's also hard to stay negative around a positive person.

Pay Attention to Body Language

Another great bully prevention tip is to help our children evaluate their body language and practice managing it. Body language does leave a lasting impact on people. Teaching our children about body language will help them control how they are affecting others. Our body gives clues to what is going on in our heart. Knowledge of body language will also give them a hand in understanding how others are genuinely feeling. They will be able to hear what's not being said. In fact, one secret to building great friendships is to understand what we are communicating with our body.

If you want to work with your child on their body language, a great place to start is with healthy hygiene habits like brushing teeth, combing hair, and bathing. Body odor, bad breath, and an unkempt appearance send messages we don't intend to send. Healthy hygiene habits make sure we don't erect walls before even starting relationships.

Want to go a step further? Try charades. Act out different emotions and see if you can guess which one the other person is imitating. Then discuss what would be appropriate ways to approach and help people experiencing those varied emotions. Make sure you talk about open and closed body language such as folded arms (closed) and arms down to the side (open). This will help them be aware of both intentional and unintentional messages they can send with the way they stand, sit, and carry themselves. Helping your child understand body language will increase their emotional intelligence and equip them for healthy relationships as they grow older.

Guiding Lights

When your kids have positive guiding lights and influences in their life, you can rest easier at night. Your child has others to look up too, to talk to, and to speak into their lives.

In today's world, children are growing up with Google and YouTube as the places where they learn whatever they want whenever they want. However, integrity, courtesy, respect, perseverance, self-control, and leadership are learned best in relationship. Google's here to stay, but the window for kids to form the habits of great character is wide open when they are young. This is when positive role models can change our children's lives and, by extension, our very own.

Let's Be Intentional

Let's imagine your child is speaking in front of their college graduating class. In their speech they are talking about the most influential people in their lives. Spend some time thinking about who these people are and how you want them to influence your family's life. You are, in essence, writing down what your children might say about them at their graduation. Use the space below to write out a description of those mentors. What type of people are they? In what ways will they influence your child's life? What will your child learn from them? How do they support your efforts as a parent?

_____

_____

_____

_____

_____

_____

_____

_____

Now go find these people. I guarantee you they are out there!

Set the Climate Control

When I was in elementary school, all the third-grade classes were given the opportunity to learn how chickens were born. Each class received a glass box with a special warming light and timer. The light was scheduled to go on and off at certain times. Add 20 eggs and some straw and the incubator set up was complete. My class's responsibility was to rotate the eggs every day. After a few weeks, however, my teacher noticed that our light had not been turning on and off at the right times. She discovered that the timer on the warming light was not working at all and we ended up with fried eggs, not cute baby chicks. We were heartbroken!

Meanwhile, the class across the hall had 20 perfectly healthy baby chicks. We all learned a valuable lesson that year. The climate of an incubator needs to be just right to hatch an egg. The artificial light, which was easily broken, produced poor results. If our little eggs would have had their mom or dad sitting on them, I bet we would have had 20 little fluffy, baby chicks, too.

In the same way, our home is the incubator for our children. A safe home is the breeding ground for great leaders and independent adults who grow to become world changers. Unsafe homes

> A safe home is the breeding ground for great leaders and independent adults who grow to become world changers.

are a breeding ground for fear and anxiety. They produce children who grow up with a lack of confidence and a lack of self-discipline. Parents are the caregivers of their home and the monitors of the home environment. It's our duty and honor as parents to protect our children. Everyday we have the opportunity to adjust the climate and create an atmosphere where our families are safe physically, emotionally, and mentally.

A house is simply a place in which you eat and sleep. A home is a place where you do family. You live, interact, rest, and enjoy each other's company. So what makes a house a home? Ultimately, the people who live in your house decide for themselves if it feels like a home. In fact, the next time you're sitting around the table having dinner together (you are having dinner together, right?), ask each family member, "What would make you feel more at home here?" Then listen. Resist the temptation to disagree or add your own thoughts. If anything, respond with, "That's good to know. Tell me more."

I've seen some kids grow up into teenagers, get their license, and never hang out at their house anymore because their house isn't a home to them. They'd rather be somewhere else that feels warmer, safer, and more connected. Imagine what could have been changed if they'd been invited into the conversation as a family and mom and dad had worked to make the home a more enjoyable place to be? Having that conversation won't magically transform your house overnight, but it is a first step that allows your family to work as a team to make the small changes that will make a big difference.

Physical Climate

In the martial arts business, we battle an invisible enemy every day. We call it the "bigfoot smell." Horrible foot odor can occur if the school is not cleaned and aired out properly on a daily basis. We have the daily task of kicking that smell monster out. We can get numb to the smell sometimes because we live and teach in the academy day in and day out. However, you can see it on our student's faces when they walk through the door and resist the urge to hold their nose. Even something as small and simple as the smell of the academy determines if our students want to be there or would rather be somewhere else. Our homes are the same way.

In contrast to that stinky foot smell, think of what you smell and how you feel walking into your favorite coffee shop. My favorite shop is warm and smells like hot chocolate. The hum of people soothes me as I slip into my favorite chair. It's a place I feel safe, relaxed, and productive as I live and work in this environment. Sometimes it's hard to get me to leave!

One of the most important aspects of physical safety in a home is literal physical safety. Home needs to be a place where we know we will not be hit, grabbed, slapped, or threatened. It should be a place where fear and anxiety are not cultivated due to "walking on eggshells" around family members. If you, as a parent, struggle with anger that is expressed physically in any way, get the help you need to learn to manage your emotions in a healthy way. Setting up a few counseling appointments is a great place to start making important changes that will increase your family's sense of safety as it relates to you.

There are three other elements to consider in the physical space. The first is simple cleanliness. I would much rather use the restroom at a coffee shop than a gas station. Your family would probably much rather spend time in a place that is clean and fresh. Cleaning goes faster when it's a family job. The other positive of taking care of the home together is that the children develop good habits they will likely carry into their adult lives.

The second element is organization. Does every item in the house have a place it belongs? Sometimes organization is challenging not because of a bad system, but because there's just too much stuff. What is your family no longer using that can be donated, recycled, or thrown away? If you need to up your game on organization, go through the house space by space and decide as a family what goes where. Work with your own style of organization though. If things are "out of sight out of mind" for you, you may find that open baskets with files work better than file drawers for paperwork.

Finally, is your house comfortable? Just like the bigfoot smell in the martial arts school, its natural to become numb to our surroundings. It's easy to get caught up in the major projects and forget about the little stuff that adds up to comfort or discomfort. We may be unaware of the cat smell, the dog hair, the locks that no longer work, or the smoke detector that hasn't had a fresh battery in years. And let's not even mention dishes and dust bunnies!

When we have the tough conversations and are willing to have fresh eyes to see each other's perspective on the house, we can begin to make changes. When the family comes together as a team, the house becomes a home, a place in which everyone enjoys spending time, and a place of safety and rest where everyone can relax and be themselves.

Emotional Climate

Are you emotionally intelligent? It may seem like an odd question to ask but emotional intelligence is really a thing. According to Dictionary.com, emotional intelligence is "the capacity to be aware of, control, and express one's emotions, and to handle interpersonal relationships judiciously and empathetically." Emotional intelligence is the key to healthy family relationships.

If we're honest most of us have some room for growth when it comes to emotional intelligence. Emotions aren't necessarily good or bad in and of themselves. They just are. It's what we do in response to those emotions or how long we sit with them that matters.

Take anger, for example. Children and grownups are both capable of anger. I experience this myself when driving in Houston traffic. I see it in students all the time when their sibling pushes all the right buttons…on purpose. Feeling the anger isn't wrong, but saying hurtful words in response or yelling at someone, those can cause divisions in a family. Why? Because words and an angry tone of voice can stick for decades. So how can we safely express our emotions in a constructive way?

One strategy we can use to help each other clearly describe our feelings and emotions is this simple sentence:
I feel _____ when _____ because _____ so I'd prefer _____.

For example, "I feel <u>embarrassed</u> when <u>you yell at me in front of my friends</u> because <u>everyone is looking at me</u> so I'd prefer <u>you come talk to me privately</u>."

This communication creates an opportunity for connection and empathy. It gives the speaker a chance to express their emotions and also provide a solution. The listener can then validate those feelings and have an idea of how to be more considerate next time. If we slow down enough and use this sentence, with a mindset to respect and honor what is shared, it protects our relationships with each other.

When a member of the family is sad, or angry, or frustrated, taking the time to empathize and recognize their emotions first protects them. According to Collin's Dictionary, empathy is "the ability to share another person's feelings and emotions as if they were your own." In the home, this looks like considering the impact your words and actions will have on the other person's emotions. It also includes telling them the impact their decisions have on your emotions. When we communicate with empathy, we make the person the priority, not the problem. We know we will have other opportunities to be understood so for now we listen and empathize. Empathy makes our home a safer place.

Another part of emotional safety is being fully present with our family. If you're anything like me, you spend too much time living in the past or planning for the future, too easily forgetting the importance of staying in the present. The power of being present really started to stick with me only a few years ago. Though my mentor's wisdom came over two decades ago, Kathy reminded me, "Appreciate your daily blessings: things like your child's goofy grin, cheek dimples, chocolate milk mustaches, bedtime stories, and hugs. When you get it wrong, forgive yourself. When you get it right, celebrate! If you don't know which one it was, grant yourself some grace. See the glass as half full and count your blessings." If she was here today, I know exactly what she would say as well: "Get off your cell phone, Newberry!"

Let's be honest, it's so easy to escape into our digital lives and forget to live and enjoy our real lives, but we have to! As a martial arts instructor, one of the biggest joys of teaching is watching a kid succeed and then celebrating with them. If I reward or compliment a student in class, the first person they look at is always mom and dad. Sometimes mom and dad are watching and give their child big smiles and thumbs up. That child's confidence skyrockets because his parents noticed and believed in him. They were *present*.

There are other times when I praise a student and we look to the parents to see what they think and the parent is on their phone or computer and missed the whole thing. It makes me sad when they miss a special moment to celebrate with their child. I know I too have missed precious moments because I was distracted by a phone. Let's agree to stay present, to be in the moment, watching for the little joys of life. Doing so creates an emotional connection and builds safety in our family.

One of the best gifts my husband gave our girls was a monthly daddy-daughter date night. He'd take one of the girls out for dinner and an activity of their choice. He did not allow himself to talk about any problems, but was intentional about being present and listening to whatever they had to say. Giving advice was only allowed when they directly asked for it. He'd open the door for them and treat them, not like children, but like princesses, giving them a foundation of how he wanted his daughters to be treated in future relationships. Many times they would come back with a special gift from daddy and to this day they have many great memories from those one-on-one dates. Intentional time spent together makes home a safe place to be.

Mental Climate

The way we think about responsibility, privileges, and mistakes makes up the mental climate of a family. How we think about these things greatly affects our children...positively or negatively. This contributes to a healthy—or unhealthy—mental climate in the home.

When home is a place for children to thrive, privileges are balanced with responsibility. As a child grows in one, they grow in the other. The privilege of getting an allowance comes with the responsibility of using money wisely to save, give, and spend. The privilege of having a pet comes with the responsibility of caring for it. The privilege of getting a new phone, tablet, or whatever the kids play with these days comes with the responsibility of following family guidelines for time spent using it.

One of my black belt students from several years back began his training as a 4-year-old. One thing I always admired about his mom was that she made him carry his own gear bag. All of his sparring equipment and weapons were packed into a taekwondo bag that was as big as he was. He trudged into the school every day with that heavy bag on his shoulders. Martial Arts was his activity, so carrying the gear bag was his responsibility. He grew up to be one tough kid, not just physically, but also mentally. He knew he could take on any challenge because he had grown up with the appropriate weight of responsibility on his shoulders that grew as he did.

The mental climate is also influenced by our approach to mistakes. One time when I was teaching a class of beginner students, I challenged them to kick higher. Some of them rose to the challenge while others didn't. One boy tried kicking so high that he fell over backwards on his bottom. In a split second I realized this was a pivotal moment. He had been faced with a challenge and he'd accepted it head on. The result was that he fell on his rear end and I could see in his face that he was embarrassed and was waiting for the class to laugh at him. He hadn't trained with me long enough to know that one thing I never allow to happen is someone to get made fun of for making a mistake.

So before the other students could react, I stopped the whole class. Pulling him to his feet, I congratulated him. *"Wow! You tried kicking so high you fell over! Some people would be too afraid of falling on their bottom to even attempt what you just attempted. You have a lot of courage. Because you are willing to take risks, I believe you will become a phenomenal black belt, or even world champion."* What could have potentially been a disastrous moment for that little boy became a proud moment. (Of course, a few minutes later I had to tell the rest of class to stop falling down on purpose and just learn the life lesson.)

Legendary basketball coach John Wooden says that, "if you're not making mistakes, then you're not doing anything." This is so true, especially in our homes. Part of the mental climate of a leader's home is that everyone understands mistakes are not only inevitable but also very valuable. Instead of punishing mistakes or avoiding them, they need to be both accepted and learned from. We'll tackle this subject a little deeper in a few pages, but for now, it's important to know that a positive perspective on mistakes is an important part of a healthy mental climate in the home.

Your Family Is a Team

We were driving through the Rocky Mountains on a recent family vacation. We were so high up we were literally driving through the clouds. The roads were narrow and winding, and to top it all off, it was pouring down rain. It was honestly the most terrifying driving experience I've ever had.

Gripping the steering wheel with white knuckles and staring at the road with intense focus, our best driver was at the wheel while our best navigator road shotgun. The other passengers sat in the back, all lights and devices turned off, silently supporting the driver in their efforts to keep the car between the white and yellow lines they could barely see in front of them.

On a crazy road trip like this, could you imagine what would happen if we allowed our children to drive the car? When they are young, they are not yet ready to take the controls of the vehicle. The same is true with the climate of the home. They are not ready yet to be in charge, yet too often we let them lead when we need to be leading. This happens when we allow their temper tantrums to get what they want just so they'll be quiet. It happens when we let our teen get away with disrespect because we don't want to deal with the struggle. Too often our children have too much control in the home.

I know from my own parenting experience how easy it is to start giving up too much control too soon. It's normal for parents to get weary of the battles. It's also natural for parents to become exhausted from the mental and emotional struggles that happen when children push boundaries and exercise their independence. When parents are tired and want to avoid the tension of the arguments, many times they'll allow their children to take over the controls and make decisions for the family. When this happens, the family becomes vulnerable because the best driver is not at the wheel.

While I'm not suggesting our kids never get the opportunity to drive the car, I am suggesting that they go through some training first. Even though they're not at the wheel yet, they are still part of the team. Creating a safe home environment that is an incubator for young leaders is a challenging task, and it's one that requires a group effort. Parents, of course, are the best ones to initiate the building of such an environment. In order to maintain this climate, every person in the house has a big responsibility. When the whole family agrees on the high value of keeping the home a safe place, then they can start working together. This is when our homes become incubators for great leaders to rest, relax, grow, and take risks.

Let's Be Intentional

When you go to the pool, there are two different kinds of people. The ones who get used to the water cannonball-style, creating waves that upset fellow swimmers, and those who slowly and gingerly lower themselves into the pool. It takes them some time, but inch by inch they get used to the water.

If you find yourself needing to change the climate of your home, I would recommend the inch by inch approach. Suddenly changing everything about the climate can be a big shock to the whole family, possibly an unpleasant one. While changing old habits with new ones can be challenging, a slow adjustment will help your whole family stay motivated as you work together to create a healthy, new normal for your family.

Need to make some climate changes? Here are a few ways to start the process. My hope is that these activities will create strong family bonds within the walls of your home.

1. **Physical climate change:** Every quarter, I bring my team on a walkthrough inspection of the martial arts school. We take note of things that need work or cleaning, and share creative ideas for how we can use the spaces differently. Your family can do a similar walkthrough of your home.

I encourage you to get the family together and go through every room of your house and take a fresh look at it. Talk about how you might use the space you have in a better way. You will be amazed at the excitement as everyone shares their ideas. Then tackle the projects one at a time. It may be a year-long process, but it's one the whole family can be involved in, creating quality family bonding time.

2. **Emotional climate change:** One evening during dinner (you are having dinner together around the table, right?) share this phrase with your family:
"I feel _____ when _____ because _____ so I'd prefer _____."

(For example, "I feel taken advantage of when you don't help clean up the kitchen after dinner because I have things I'd also like to do in the evening so I'd prefer you help me clear the table and get the kitchen cleaned up before you go on to your after dinner activities.")

Explain why it's an important way to communicate and then role play how to use it. Have each family member give the phrase a spin. You might encourage them to think of a recent time they were frustrated by something or someone and to think of that situation and turn their frustration into communication.

3. **Mental climate change:** Make a sign that reminds your family of how you will think about each other or mistakes. Several years ago my oldest daughter gave me a gift, and now it's one of my favorite things hanging on my kitchen wall. The simple "We Do" phrases written across the canvas in elegant font

remind me of the type of home in which I want my family to live.

You can create a "we do" canvas to hang in a highly visible room in your home. Get your whole family involved in deciding the phrases makes it a reminder and commitment for everyone.

My poster says:

> In this house we do SECOND CHANCES.
>
> We do REAL, We do GRACE, We do MISTAKES.
>
> We do I'M SORRIES, We do HUGS.
>
> We do FAMILY, We do LOVE.

Avoid the Potholes

It was a rare occurrence in the Newberry household. All three of my teen and adult daughters were ready to head out the door for a family get-together we were headed to. Realizing that my husband was still making some final preparations, they all three plopped themselves down on the oversized olive green couch that sits in a corner of our living room. They sat there next to each other, lost in conversation.

I couldn't believe it. Their makeup? Done. Their hair? Fixed. Their coats? Bundled tight, ready to walk out the door at a moment's notice.

If you're the parent of multiple girls, you know this is not the way it usually plays out. Usually there's a declaration of, "Wait! I'm just going to take a really fast shower," five minutes before the predetermined departure time. Or a last minute request to raid your shoe closet because they have, "Nothing that goes with this outfit." Or a shout, "Let me have the front seat! I need to put my face on!" while mascara wands fly.

I was impressed and ready to head out the door before they changed their mind. "What are we waiting for?" I asked. "Eagle Scout is getting his stuff in the car," my middle daughter, Tiffany, declared with a smirk.

My husband, Jeff, has earned himself the nickname 'Eagle Scout' by the girls because he is known to go to painstaking lengths to be prepared for *anything*. The girls poke fun at him for all he does before he leaves the house, until they realize that they've forgotten something and Dad *always* has the thing they need.

Maybe it's his upbringing with parents who taught him the importance of discipline and preparation. Maybe it's his experience as a police officer for thirteen years. Maybe it's that he really is an Eagle Scout. Whatever it is that motivates him, Jeff makes sure he is prepared for whatever could possibly be thrown his way. Sometimes, he's overly prepared, and sometimes we all avoid a lot of frustration and pain because of his preparedness.

Before we backed out of the driveway that snowy Thursday night, Jeff:

- Packed the car with his bags of "essentials" that we may have needed.
- Checked the weather to see what we were driving into.
- Entered our destination into his GPS even though he knew exactly how to get there.
- Made sure the car had gas.
- Asked us girls if we had everything.

Sure, my girls may poke a little fun at my husband for his over-caution, but the truth is that his "essentials" have helped us out of a jam on more than one occasion. Once at a hotel, Tiffany, the same daughter who poked a little fun at "Eagle Scout," was saved by his preparedness when she dropped her glasses and the frames loosened. She put her crooked glasses on her face and let out an exasperated sigh. Jeff reached into his bag of essentials and handed her an eyeglass repair kit. Her sigh turned into a squeal and she announced, "Yes! Dad! Your boy scout stuff paid off!"

Being prepared may not help create the perfect set of circumstances, but it sure can help us avoid a lot of painful ones. When we adopt the same kind of mindset in parenting, we're intentional about preparing our kids for the future. Making preparations to build their character and habits may not promise them a life of perfect circumstances, but it sure can help them avoid a lot of painful ones.

As influencers of the next generation, we have the responsibility to equip our children with their own set of tools. This preparation helps them to avoid the pitfalls that threaten their futures and the potholes that could cause a flat tire along the way. Let's explore the tools—they all start with C—that we can teach them to pack in their bag of "essentials" and the corresponding potholes both we and they need to avoid along the journey.

Connection

The greatest, most impactful leaders are those whose anchor is chained to their purpose and whose sails are moved by satisfaction and fulfillment—not just a desire to blindly follow a generic dream of life success. If we want our kids to be effective leaders, we have to guide them to discover the fulfillment of a purpose-driven life at an early age. We have to connect them to their purpose rather than the American Dream.

This is a challenge for many of us because we didn't do that ourselves. Many of us followed someone else's expectations rather than exploring our own passions, dreams, and purpose. So how can we lead our kids differently? How can we teach them that those feelings of passion are the ones they need to chase after and pursue?

First, we can help our children to identify their interests and invest in them. When your child finds something that sparks a fire and passion within them, press into it with them, even if it's not what you have imagined or even think will actually become their ultimate purpose. For example, if your son takes a liking to the debate team and he's wildly interested and passionate about it, encourage it! Maybe he'll be a lawyer. Maybe he'll be a politician. Or maybe he'll be neither of those things, but the assertiveness he hones in the craft of debate will equip him for his ultimate purpose that is yet unknown. Regardless of the eventual role debate will play in his life, teaching him what it feels like to chase hard after his passions is one of the greatest gifts you can give him. Once he feels what it's like to pour himself into what he loves, he'll be better able to identify what he doesn't love—and be less tempted to pursue it.

Second, we can commit to modeling our own lives as an example. We can pursue our own purposes with passion—and explain every step of the process as we do. The more familiar and comfortable our children can become with purpose-driven lives, the more normal it will become to them, and the more likely they will be to duplicate it. Nothing can teach a lesson with conviction quite like a life led by example, so let's lead one.

It wouldn't make sense to get in the car with no destination in mind, and it doesn't make sense to live an average life with no purpose in mind. Our children will be far more effective leaders when they know where they're going, so let's help them connect the dots to discovering their destination as early as possible. Trust me, when you do that, having a front row seat for their "take-off" will be the best seat in the house.

Confidence

One of the most tempting potholes on the journey of empowering our kids for success is to not only take over the steering wheel of their lives, but deploy the airbags, too—just in case. As loving as it may seem at times, we have to resist the desire to protect our kids from every pain, failure, and struggle because sometimes our desire to protect at all costs has the opposite effect. In fact, it's incredibly dangerous.

If we're constantly stepping in to rescue our kids at the last minute, saving them from a rough landing, we're taking away the lesson that their natural consequence would have taught. Pain, as difficult as it is to watch, is a great teacher. If we're going to watch our kids experience failure, discomfort, and even painful consequences from their decisions, it's best to allow those lessons to happen when they're young rather than when they're out on their own and the stakes are greater. Our job is to build confidence rather than keeping our child wrapped in bubble wrap.

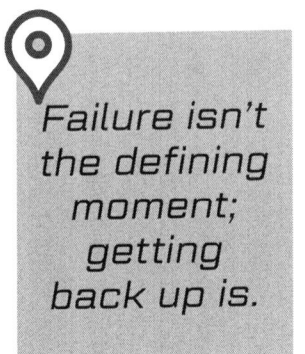

> Failure isn't the defining moment; getting back up is.

Have you ever watched a baby chick peck out of its shell? It's such a difficult process to watch. They peck for a while and stop. Then they peck some more and rest. It can sometimes take 24 hours or more! Did you also know that if you help them they may die? That's right. The hard work of pecking actually makes them stronger. So if we rob them of a strength-building opportunity, we're not really helping them. In the same way, overprotection actually weakens our children and steals away opportunities for them to try, fail, try again, growing in confidence and strength in the process.

Go ahead, let failure be their professor. Just don't let them stay defeated. Lift their chins, whisper their worth, and remind them that **failure is just an instance, not an identity. Failure isn't the defining moment, getting back up is.**

Compassion

We live in a me-first society. One of a parent's biggest challenge is making sure our kids are others-focused. Allowing them to believe that the world revolves around them is a dangerous, and increasingly common, pothole we must avoid.

I've seen firsthand the effects on young adults when they learn that the world is far less concerned with their feelings than their parents were—and it can all be avoided if we simply teach our children that the foundation of leadership is servanthood. This foundation will serve them well in marriage, as a parent, in friendship, and in their life's work. You see, a leader is really just a head servant; the visionary through whom many benefit. *That's* the kind of leader we want to develop. Without instilling compassion, a conceited leader can quickly become a dictator.

Our job is to grow compassion and resist the me-first ways that grow conceit. We have to find ways for our child to serve others and make others a priority. When our children participate in others-focused, service-based activities, they develop a compassion that will fuel their future purposes. Because the last thing we want is for them to be so self-absorbed that by the time they reach the destination of success, they realize they never looked up long enough to soak in the journey.

Communication

We've all been on that road trip from you know where. Everyone's been in the car for far too long, irritability rises, and tolerance falls. Grumpy attitudes quickly turn into yelling matches and all sensible communication flies out the window. If our kids suppress their communication, and it goes unnoticed for too long, they can quickly explode with emotion much like shortened fuses. Often, kids without an outlet to express their emotion internalize their stress and inner conflict to a point that they start to repeat their self-criticism on a loop in their minds. Failing to meet the unrealistic expectations they set for themselves (or that culture or family has encouraged them to have), convinces them that they've fallen short in some way, and that becomes their self-talk.

Is your family a safe place for emotion? Is it safe for expressing frustration appropriately? Can family members disagree and still respect each other? If we don't want our kids to go internally with self-criticism or explode when they just can't hold things in any more, we have to make our home a safe place to communicate thoughts and feelings even if they're different than ours.

As a parent, our job is also to notice the nonverbal indications that something is weighing heavily on our child and help them process it. When addressed early, we can intervene on their behalf and help them identify feelings and struggles when they don't know how to do that themselves. Learning how to identify and effectively communicate emotions respectfully will have lifetime benefits for our kids and their future relationships.

Collaboration

There is a quote that has become an anthem of sorts among leaders. "If you want something done right, you have to do it yourself." While it sounds very empowering, the truth is this is a very damaging perspective. If we teach our kids that the only way to do something efficiently is to refuse help and figure out how to be an expert at everything themselves, we're setting them up for failure for sure. We have to encourage collaboration over isolation.

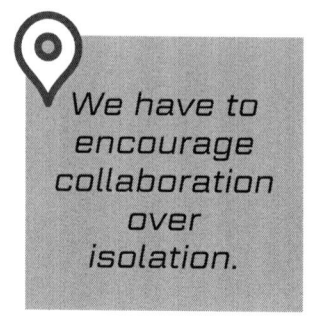

> We have to encourage collaboration over isolation.

Think of our road trip analogy. When my family and I travel, we all bring something unique to the table. I make the arrangements for where we're going to stay. My husband, Jeff, packs the car. My oldest daughter, Melanie, considers everyone's favorite things and makes an itinerary of activities. Her husband, Seth, always finds the best restaurants and plans our meals. Tiffany, my middle daughter, gets the grandkids packed and ready to go, and her husband, Cesar, makes the plans for entertainment (often, he IS the entertainment). Destani, my youngest daughter, gets the snacks for the family and we're ready to go. How much more miserable of a process would arranging for a family trip be if we didn't all work together? And how much more miserable of a time will our kids have as independent adults if they never learn to contribute to a team?

Rather than encouraging our kids to be islands—navigating this life alone—let's teach them to contribute, to delegate, and to collaborate. Let's encourage them to build community and recognize there is power in teamwork. Sometimes these type of social skills aren't just naturally learned, and we have to make a concentrated effort to teach them along the way. We do that best by living in community ourselves, allowing our kids a front row seat at what teamwork looks like in everyday life: helping neighbors, asking friends to help with a project, being part of a small group at church, serving on committees at school. As our kids get older, we need to encourage them to participate in school clubs, scouting programs, mission trips, and community service activities that help them see that more can be accomplished together than apart.

Critical Thinking

Once, when Olivia was a young girl, her dad let her tell him the directions on how to get to her aunt's house. At one point, Olivia told him to take the wrong turn and knowing it was wrong, he took it anyway. They were three miles down the road going the wrong way when she realized her mistake and had to get them back on track. He could have corrected Olivia himself and took the right turn, but instead he let her figure it out and solve the problem.

As a parent, this story really stood out to me. How often do we see our kids making a mistake and immediately correct them before they ever realized it was a mistake? How often do we solve their problems for them? And more soberly, what are they going to do when they're on their own and have no protection from us? We need to encourage critical thinking rather than jumping in with parent-led problem-solving.

Learning how to think critically and to creatively solve problems is one of the greatest gifts we can give our kids. Then, when they're faced with unique problems and circumstances, they can think through them to find a solution. Really great leaders are the ones called on to do just that when others can't. Let's equip them to be the leaders in those situations.

Creativity

When traveling for a long period of time with kids, we had to get creative on ways to entertain. I Spy, the alphabet road trip game, telling stories, singing funny songs: these were all utilized on our family's many road trips. Those tactics turned long and boring car rides into moments of humor, bonding, and great memories.

Creativity is needed and allowed on road trips, but what about in everyday life? Are you allowing your kids to swim upstream in a downstream world or are you afraid of your kids standing out in some way and not representing you or your family well if they do so? Sometimes we keep our kids in boxes they long to break out of everyday. Their ideas may not seem logical or even make sense with current knowledge but they may be the next inventor, the next CEO, or the next President who is an out-of-the-box-thinker and able to make an incredible impact on society.

Let your child try other sports, explore multiple interests, and make friends with people of other cultures. Let her challenge current thinking and come up with fresh ideas. Give him a broken computer and let him tear it apart and figure out how things work. God didn't use cookie cutters when He created the world, and we shouldn't teach our kids that they have to be what everyone else wants to be either. They have limitless potential. Let's help them tap into it because the sky's the limit!

Teaching Leadership as a Life Passion

For the past three decades, I have been dedicated to teaching leadership and life skills through martial arts. Seven years ago I decided I believed so strongly in the concept that I changed the name of my martial arts academy to "Leaders for Life". I went on a journey of growth and discovery, trying to find the character and skills that children were missing out on in their formal education. I studied the education systems of countries all over the world. I read what other parents were reading about parenting. I focused in on the families in my taekwondo school, trying to teach the lessons that would resonate with them the most.

The result of that journey is the seven C's we just laid out for you in this chapter. These are the skills I wish I had learned sooner. These are the skills I wish for every student that walks through the doors of my academy to learn. These are the lessons I will speak about, teach about, and write about for the rest of my life because I believe they can have an incredible, lasting impact on our lives. When our children grow up in an environment of leadership and are equipped with these skills, they'll be ready to stand up to life's challenges. They will be ready to lead and change their own corner of the world for the better.

Let's Be Intentional

Depending on the age of your child, what are some creative ways you can start teaching them each of the seven C's? What are some ways your child can practice? How will you measure your child's level of progress in developing these valuable life skills? Use the space on the next page to write out some thoughts and next steps for one of the C's. Then use a notebook to flesh out next steps for the other C's.

**Connection | Confidence | Compassion
Communication | Collaboration
Critical Thinking | Creativity**

Life Skill: _____

How can I teach this life skill to my child? _____

_____

_____

_____

_____

How can I help them practice this life skill? _____

_____

_____

_____

_____

How will I know they have learned and internalized this life skill? _____

_____

_____

_____

_____

_____

_____

Welcome Mistakes

I have spent most of my adult life running martial arts academies and working with children and families to instill leadership in children. Most days I prefer to be on the mat teaching, but sometimes I have opportunities to sit down and chat in the office with families who are currently experiencing a unique challenge. Some of those meetings over the years remain fresh and clear in my memories.

I remember one particular Monday when I had two appointments back to back and both involved students who were having trouble at school. Family #1 marched into my office and practically oozed frustration and disappointment. They were incredibly upset at their son because he had mouthed off and rolled his eyes at a teacher. As they sat their son down in front of me, the parents launched into a five-minute explanation of how angry they were at this little boy's behavior. I know they didn't realize it but in their anger they ridiculed and demoralized their child. It seemed they wanted me to affirm their judgment and continue the verbal bombardment. I honestly think they believed this approach of anger and criticism

> "Take chances, make mistakes. That's how you grow. Pain nourishes your courage. You have to fail in order to practice being brave."
>
> Mary Tyler Moore

would ensure that this little boy would learn his lesson and never make the same mistake twice.

It seemed clear to me that all this child was learning was that mistakes are unacceptable and that the result would be embarrassment and condemnation. Through the whole meeting, the little boy was slumped over in defeat. Though I tried, his parents did not give me a chance to talk to their son. All they wanted me to know was "what kind of disappointing child I was dealing with." My heart broke for that little boy, and I only saw him for a few more classes before his parents withdrew him from our program because "karate was not working for him."

As disheartening as that meeting was, my next appointment was a breath of fresh air. Family #2 came into my office and sat down. Their little boy was about the same age as my earlier appointment and he was not happy about being there. The parents calmly asked him to share what happened at school that day. I began to encourage him with probing questions and soon enough the story came out that he had lost a bet and had "peed a circle around the bathroom walls." He got caught and was suspended from school for a day. This surprised the socks off me because he was one of my best students.

He confessed his foolishness all the while unable to even look me in the eye. Then he waited for my reaction, tense and ashamed. "Well, that's a new one for me," I said. "That's a big mistake. At least you kept your word and made good on your bet. So what did you learn out of this whole thing?"

This family and I then spent the next several minutes dissecting the life lessons that could be gleaned from the situation. The little boy assured me he would not accept another harmful bet or "pee in a ring around the wall." We all agreed on the consequence that he would not test for his next belt until he repaid the damage to the school and apologized to his principal and teacher. Fast forward a couple years and this same child became one of our best Junior Leaders, and we've chuckled together many times over his life lesson.

In martial arts, if you are in a confrontation, the first thing I would tell you is to "cover up." This means putting up your hands up around your head in order to protect your brain and face. In self-defense it is vitally important to protect our head. This is why "cover up" is so important. The same thing is true when we are intentionally raising our children to be leaders. The most vulnerable position our children will be in mentally is when they make a mistake. We get the honor of protecting their minds until they are strong enough to recognize their own vulnerabilities and protect themselves. Let's explore exactly how to do that.

Mistakes Welcome

It's very easy for both children and adults to withdraw and lose confidence when they make a mistake. It's also entirely possible for a mistake to be a springboard for personal growth and future victory. This is why, when we teach martial arts, we encourage our students to make mistakes and make them often. The outcome all depends on how the mistake is addressed.

Let's take a closer look at the two different approaches to handling mistakes that are illustrated in the stories about the two little boys. With the first incident, it was clear to me that the child was ridiculed for his mistake and it resulted in shame and embarrassment and no doubt a growing feeling of distrust towards the adults in his life. The few times he did come back to class, he would not try hard or want to stand out in any way. I still believe to this day that he was avoiding any kind of contact with me because he was hiding from the embarrassment of how he was treated in front of me.

I saw that young man years later and, not surprisingly, his self image was very low. The way he carried himself spoke volumes as he seemed to feel he was not good at anything and that he would not amount to much. Of course, that was far from the truth. Even though I only had a few opportunities to teach him, I could see incredible amounts of talent and potential inside him. Sadly, though, the only thing he could see was that he was painful failure.

The second boy's parents allowed him to feel the weight of his decision and own it. They gave him some grace and forgave the infraction. They also approached his mistake as a learning opportunity. Recognizing that he could do something to correct his behavior now allowed him to know there could be a different outcome the next time he was put under negative peer pressure. The meeting was wrapped up in words of wisdom about the situation to help the child see his mistake was not a permanent failure, but rather a springboard for an even better future.

These two boys were treated very differently. As a result, one boy withdrew, and the other excelled. One boy was loved with conditions, and other was unconditionally loved. As parents, we have to know the difference, love well, and expect mistakes to happen.

The way others react when children make a mistake has a deep impact on their minds. They collect data from these reactions and start to form stories about who they are and what they are capable of. Harsh words of frustration, shock, or disappointment can cause a child to believe stories that simply aren't true such as, "I'm no good at this," or, "I'm so stupid," or even, "I'm a failure."

These stories affect every area of their lives, mind, emotions, spiritual views, bodies, and relationships. If the false stories in our minds linger too long, our relationships can be seriously damaged as a result. However, if the stories we tell ourselves are positive, it affects us positively, and our relationships are strengthened and deepened.

Our reactions to our child's mistakes and failure carry a deep and lasting impact. This is why we need to welcome mistakes. Yep, you read that right. *We need to welcome mistakes.* Expect them. Embrace them. Make your home a safe place for mistakes to happen.

Welcoming mistakes is not the same as overlooking them. As parents, it's our responsibility to highlight and correct their mistakes so our child can glean life lessons and know how to make better choices the next time they're in a similar situation. Mistakes are inevitable, but intentional parenting uses mistakes to our child's advantage.

> We need to welcome mistakes.

How do we do that practically? There are three keys that will help your family welcome mistakes and leverage them for growth: compassion, connection, and correction. These three components restore our relational health and heal the spirit when failure is screaming we're not worthy of love and are not capable of leadership. We counteract the shame of a failure by covering the embarrassment with **compassion**. We bridge the separation caused by the mistake by drawing near with **connection**. Then we prevent future mistakes of the same nature by gently **correcting** and guiding our children in the way they should go. Let's look at each of these more closely.

Compassion

> Compassion is choosing to love someone on their worst day just as much as we love them on their best day.

Compassion is choosing to love someone on their worst day just as much as we love them on their best day. When we model compassion for our children, they are growing up with the best example of what unconditional love looks like. So how do we show compassion? What does it look like? It's being patient when they are impatient, remaining calm when they are frustrated, and generously giving grace when mistakes are made. One of the best ways to reassure your child with compassion is to tell them that there is nothing they can do that will make you stop loving them.

There is a great sense of confidence and strength that comes when we know someone will never stop loving us, especially when we make mistakes. In this way, compassion gives our relationships an upgrade to something deeper and more genuine. Their confidence in our unconditional love will give them the courage to bring their mistakes to us instead of hiding them from us. Compassion gives our children memories of *love* instead of *embarrassment*.

Connection

When we make mistakes, one of the first things we want to do is withdraw. This is because life has taught us we should be ashamed. And often times we would rather hide than expose our shame. We hope that the distance we create between us and the mistake will make the memories of it less painful.

Children don't realize that the one thing that will make them feel better and help the situation is reconnecting with the people who love them the most. If we are a safe person for them to fail with, children will learn to seek comfort from people. If we're not a safe person for them to fail with, our children will seek comfort from things. Seeking comfort from relationships is much healthier—and honestly some of us adults have trouble with that as well because we didn't grow up in an environment in which it was safe to fail. Learning to be a safe place for your kids failure can also be a growth place for yourself.

Having honest and open communication without anger and shame will help the healing and learning process. Quick recovery is key. If they spill milk, give them a rag; when they make a mistake, give them forgiveness and connection.

In the martial arts, space is escape and contact is control. When we want to get away from a dangerous situation, we are naturally wired to escape. If we know we are going to be safe, however, we will create contact. Our children are the same way. When our children feel safe and secure in their environment, they will connect with their parents. If they don't feel secure, they will create distance and disconnect from their family. This is a great evaluation tool to measure how our children feel about their relationship with us. Do they create space or make contact?

One of the best ways to encourage our children to draw close is for us to learn to control our response to their mistakes. If children fear a parent reacting in shock or outrage when they mess up, their gut instinct will be to hide from you by lying or attempting to cover up the mistake. If they know you will react calmly when they admit a mistake and help them learn and make it right, they will be far more apt to come to you when they mess up.

Correction

When a student messes up In a martial arts class, we train our instructors to use positive correction rather than criticism to get that student back on the right track. This process starts with them approaching the student in private, never in public. The instructor begins by complimenting the student for something they did well. Then they make the correction and follow it up with praise when the student applies and changes their behavior. We call this the correction sandwich where you sandwich correction between two pieces of praise. The initial praise opens the student up to receiving correction. The follow up praise reinforces the positive behavior or technique change and encourages them to repeat the change to eventually form a new habit. As parents, we can and need to use the same communication at home.

Correcting our children is rarely pleasant, for either parent or child, but it's necessary for them to change their behavior. It's a difficult, but beautiful, act of love to gently correct. We love them too much to allow them to continue behaving in a way that will damage their relationships and life opportunities both now and in the future.

Discipline is simply allowing children to experience the promised consequence of their choices. Explain to your child that every choice they make comes with either a reward or consequence. If they choose well, they receive the reward. If they choose poorly, they experience the promised consequence. "I'm sorry, darling, but you chose to disobey so now I have to discipline you because I love you too much to allow you to continue behaving that way."

What's the Difference Between Discipline and Punishment?

A beautiful piece of advice I've gleaned over the years from watching and working closely with many wonderful parents is this: Always discipline out of love, never punish out of frustration. I must confess I have done it both ways as a parent and the first has always been more effective.

> *Always discipline out of love.*

Let me illustrate with a story: little James came into my office to chat. He was smiling cheerfully and continued to beam up at me as he relayed why he had gotten in trouble. His 5-year-old explanation started with this: "I got in trouble because I threw a fit."

"I know you got in trouble, but why was it bad to throw a fit?" I probed gently, wanting to see how much he understood.

"Because I was bad," was his simple answer.

"Okay, but James, why was it bad to throw a fit?"

"I don't know."

I realized in that moment that the best thing I could do to help James was not to sternly chastise him, but rather to help him comprehend why it was bad. I explained that when he throws a fit, he loses his self-control. When we lose our self control, sometimes we say or do things that hurt other people. I asked him what would happen if he was playing with a friend and got angry and lost self-control.

"I might hurt them and they may not play with me anymore," was his answer. The light bulb had slowly turned on in his young mind. In a small way, he was beginning to understand how his behavior affected his relationships. He was beginning to understand the value of self-control.

When a child behaves poorly and we react in frustration, the child usually receives instant punishment because we want the bad behavior to stop. All the child learns from this style of correction is that their behavior was bad and resulted in punishment, but their young minds cannot always connect all the dots. They don't understand WHY what they did was wrong. They only know not to repeat it because they don't want to get in trouble or make mom or dad angry.

Let me clarify that their behavior may make you angry. However, that's not when we need to correct. In their book ***No More Perfect Kids***, Dr. Kathy Koch and Jill Savage remind us that, "Loving deeply means allowing kids to make mistakes without the consequence of our anger.[3]" Your child probably needs a consequence but your anger is not an effective consequence for their poor choices.

When we take a moment to pause and breathe before correcting our children, we can more effectively express compassion,

---

[3] Savage, Jill, and Kathy Koch. *No More Perfect Kids: Love Your Kids for Who They Are*. Moody Publishers, 2014. Pg 194.

connect with their heart, and correct in a way that let's us explain the why. When they understand the WHY, the life lesson and correction have a more positive and deeper impact. And as a bonus, we actually don't have to correct them as often!

Our words matter. Our expectation of mistakes matters. Our self-control matters. As we use the three keys of compassion, connection, and correction we create an environment that is emotionally safe, allows for failure, and equips a child to gain wisdom from their mistakes.

Let's Be Intentional

Take a few moments to ponder the following questions and consider how well your family has established the three discipline keys of compassion, connection, and correction. If this is new information to you, remember it's never too late to start doing the right thing!

Compassion

1. Do my children know that I love them unconditionally?
2. How often do I tell them that nothing they do could make me stop loving them?
3. Do they know their mistakes will not be the topic of my conversations with friends?

Connection

1. Do my kids know I would rather them tell the truth then hide a secret?

2. Am I safe in my responses for them to bring their mistakes to me?
3. Do my children often come to me for advice?
4. Do I take time to connect with my children on a daily basis? (listening, games, hugs, parent/child date nights, etc.)

Correction

1. Do I avoid majoring on a minor or minoring on a major? (In other words, do I make too big a deal about a small infraction or avoid dealing with a problem that could lead to major future struggles?)
2. Do my children know what the rewards and consequences will be for their choices?
3. Do I say what I do and do what I say? (In other words, do my children know that I don't bluff when warning them of consequences?)

PART THREE

A TRIP OF A LIFETIME

9 Launch a Confident Leader

It was almost my turn to recite a spelling word in front of my whole third grade class. The anxiety caused my chest to tighten and my breath became short and shallow. Droplets of sweat began to form above my lip and the heat of my thick exhale seemed to fit right in with the thick humid air of the classroom.

The expression on my classmates' faces slowly changed as each one grasped the spelling lesson our teacher was teaching. Not mine. I desperately wanted to experience that "ah ha!" moment. The thought of doing so was subtle, yet almost tangible. It was enticing, but elusive. I wanted to experience it for myself, but comprehension seemed to be always just past my reach.

Now, despite my silent pleading with the clock to tick faster and the bell to ring sooner, it was my turn. "Tina, I need you to spell the word 'pretty,'" my teacher commanded from her desk which sat perched on an elevated platform in the middle of the classroom.

"P-U—"

"No," my teacher interrupted, indicating I had made a mistake.

"P-U-R—"

"No, Tina. Try again," she commanded.

"P-R-U—"

"No. How can you not know how to spell this word?" She said as she leaned over her desk on the platform to peer down at mine just in front of her. "You have blonde hair and blue eyes, and you don't know how to spell the word pretty? You come sit on top of my desk until you figure it out."

I stood up from my chair reluctantly and climbed up and sat on her desk, legs dangling over the side. *I'm trying. Can't she see that? I'm sounding it out the way I'm supposed to. P-U-R-T-Y. Is that right? No. Two T's. I know it has two T's. P-U-R-T-T-Y.*

I sat on top of her desk for what felt like forever. I peered down at my classmates hoping to secure a hint on how to spell the word, but honestly I'd just settle for a drop of compassion in their eyes. "Don't help her," my teacher commanded the other students.

After several more silent minutes passed, she instructed the other students to get their lunches and prepare for indoor recess as I sat on the desk, humiliated. *Will I not be able to eat or play today? What will my dad do when I tell him about this? Surely this cannot be okay.*

As the other students hustled their way through our way-too-crowded classroom, I thought, *"One day, I will create a place where no child ever feels like this—a place where humiliation won't be allowed."* This became fuel for my dream and would change the trajectory of my life forever. I don't remember exactly how that day turned out. In fact, there are probably a lot of days spent in the suburbs of Washington DC that have left my memory, but that traumatic episode is forever ingrained in my mind. Looking back, I can now see all the clues that were missed in my education.

Like the days that I cried out to my parents in frustration because I couldn't understand why everything at school was so much harder for me. I was trying. I was staying late to get extra help with homework, but nothing was working. I just couldn't understand. I can remember the expressions on my parents faces as I begged to understand why I was different. As an adult, I now know those expressions were disappointment in a difficult situation, but to my nine-year-old self, I registered those expressions to mean I was a disappointment.

Then there were the days I got pulled out of class for "testing." I didn't know what I was being tested for, but I knew I didn't like it. Those days resulted in my parents whispering with my teacher as they tried to make sense of my inability to differentiate the value of a four and a seven, how I repeatedly thought a three was an eight, or the 'dancing letters' I described as I tried to read.

Finally there was a day when I sat alone in a chair in the school hallway as my parents discussed what dyslexia would mean for my future. They explained my learning disability to me and told me my brain would always work differently. They also explained that while people with dyslexia live with comprehension problems, they also tend to be fiercely creative and will learn to adapt to other learning styles. I was then sent to special education classes that were supposed to help me. However, with the whispers from the other children, I began to suspect "different" really meant "dumb." With all of the extra study practice and additional assignments, I was often pulled out of the extracurricular activities that would encourage and ignite my creative side—one of the few natural blessings that came with my dyslexia diagnosis.

The country was going through a lot of political changes at that time and our neighborhood was becoming unsafe. These reasons combined with my education difficulties brought my parents to a difficult decision. My grandparents lived in central Illinois and told my parents that the schools were better and had smaller class sizes. They assured them that I would be able to get the help I needed. So my parents took the risk. They chose to move us out of Washington, D.C. and make our home in Mattoon, Illinois.

Yes, I walked a difficult childhood with memories that left emotional scars that healed slowly, but here's what I love about my story: my parents intentionally made changes so the direction of my story would change for the better. After those difficult days, my parents got ahead of my problem and refused to see my dyslexia as a life-sentence. The lessons I learned as they helped me overcome those challenges have molded me into the person I am today, equipped by hard experience to help others walk similar paths and thrive, not merely survive.

The move to Illinois was a pivotal point in my life. In my new school I was encouraged to thrive in creative environments and excel within physical outlets. I was able to cultivate my strengths which helped me overcome my weaknesses. My parents put teachers, mentors, coaches, and instructors in my life who came alongside me to rebuild my confidence. They empowered me to believe there was no challenge bigger than my determination—as long as I refused to stay defeated. Sure, my childhood came with challenges, but without them, I never would have grown my grit. I would also never have been introduced to martial arts, which took all the lessons I was learning and brought them to a new level of impact and application.

Confidence from the Inside Out

When I was 12, my father enrolled himself in a local martial arts class in our new hometown. He saw not only the benefits for himself, but the benefits for all of our family. At age 14, after months of convincing me, he enrolled me in the martial arts school, too.

I'll never forget my first day. To say it wasn't love at first sight would be an understatement! I was not only reluctant but also defiant. Both of those were fueled by my lack of confidence. I still felt defective because of my dyslexia. Thankfully, my father recognized the benefits of martial arts as not only physical fitness and self-defense, but also instilling confidence and self-discipline at the same time. This was also an activity we could do as a family, so he pushed until I caved.

My father and I came to an agreement that I would try martial arts for six months. Both my parents and my instructors worked together to increase my confidence. When I was a yellow belt, and my six month agreement was almost up, my instructor told me I had to go to a tournament. My confidence deficit screamed inside my head that this was a bad idea, but my wise mentors had already piqued my competitive nature. They taught me how to set a goal and take small, measurable steps towards those goals. Because the tournament was something physical and competitive, I actually excelled at it. Martial arts suddenly became a beacon of hope for me. I began to realize this was something I could be really, really good at.

What I didn't realize is that this combination of having great mentors, learning how to set goals, and achieving results also increased my confidence. Great mentors, teachers, and martial arts instructors teach the leadership lessons and life skills that are shared on the pages of this book. Can you imagine the impact you'll have if your child hears these principles both at home and in the outside world?

In martial arts, we teach children to look and act like confident leaders. We teach them to carry themselves by standing up straight, shoulders back, chin up, and voice projected. We teach our students these ways to demonstrate confidence because, as Tony Robbins says, "motion creates emotion." Even a small change like standing up straight and meeting people's eyes can grow a child's confidence. This outward confidence we teach our students is extremely valuable, but it's only half the story. The other half is what is happening inside their minds and inside their homes.

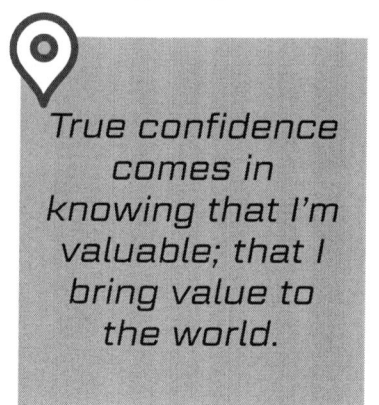

> True confidence comes in knowing that I'm valuable; that I bring value to the world.

When I was a child, I didn't feel valuable at all. When it comes to worth, children can sit in shame as I did or swing over to the other side with pride. Shame happens when a child struggles and wishes they were invisible. Pride happens when our kids grow up thinking the world revolves around them. Confidence sits in the middle of those two extremes. In fact, the balance of true confidence comes in knowing that I'm valuable, and I bring value to the world.

It's our job as parents to teach our children confidence from the inside out. I can teach a confident posture at my academy, but parents get the opportunity to instill inner confidence at home. Outward confidence without the inward source will fade out eventually, or, worse yet, turn these children towards bullying actions or self-harm in attempts to fix their own dwindling view of their worth. A true sense of incredible worth is what happens when outward and inward confidence are working in sync.

Children come with a sense of purpose already inside of them. Just ask any child what they want to be when they grow up, and you'll hear about their dreams of being police officers, superheroes, doctors, and firefighters! They are filled with a desire for adventure, a sense of anticipation, and limitless creativity. Everything they need to be leaders comes pre-programmed inside of them. Leadership is a birthright to children. Then the lies come along and diminish their potential. To release the superstar status they already have inside them, we have to help set them free from lies.

In order to create leaders for life, we have to teach them how to recognize the lies for themselves, and then replace those lies with truth. When they can identify and replace the lies on their own, they should be able to live out authentic confidence as adults when they fly from your nest.

Limit Lies with Transforming Truth

Our children have the heart, determination, and hope of a superhero, yet too often they settle for something much less. Lies move their visions of grandeur to a limited reality. Lies change risk takers into risk avoiders. Lies move confident boys and girls to fearful, anxious children. All lies fuel worry, doubt, and fear and they are the killers of dreams and possibilities.

The source of the strength for overcoming lies is a deep sense of true worth. We help our children discover their worth when we cultivate the gifts and abilities within them and remind them that making a mistake doesn't mean they are a mistake. We also help them understand that practically using their gifts and talents on purpose for a purpose grows confidence and, eventually, has the power to change the world.

The challenge is raising a child who is confident, but not arrogant or prideful. We want them to be both confident and humble. When they have this delicate balance, they are positioned to be of service to their community and world.

In my martial arts academy, one strategy I use to get the students' attention is to yell out, "Eyes on who?" And they respond, "Eyes on you." You see, what we give attention to is also where we get our strength. My students look to their instructors for strength, guidance, and acceptance. They represent possibility. Too many times in life we give our attention to the problem instead of focusing on the possibilities.

Will you do your part to raise a generation of leaders who know how to identify confidence killers and replace them with confidence builders? We live in a world full of anxiety and depression. This too often comes from listening to lies until they become the invisible shapers of our lives. We have the opportunity to be a generation of parents who are vigilant about stomping out lies and exchanging them for confidence-building truth.

How do we do this? First we recognize the lie and call it what it is: a blatant falsehood that has no place determining our worth or potential. Then we root it out and replace it with the truth. This is the part of the process that takes time. The deeper the lie, the longer it takes to dig out all the deep roots it's dug into our hearts. If we catch the lie sooner, it's far easier to pull it out. This is why intentional parents are vigilant about exploring their children's' internal thought processes.

This, of course, is no easy task. Some children can and will express their feelings freely. Others internalize emotions and require you to play detective. Watch their interaction with others and pay attention to what is happening on their social media pages. Spend time with them alone going on "Daddy Date Nights" or "Mom and Me Dates". This is time to listen (NOT give advice), ask questions, and speak their love language. It's time to feel what they are feeling. In this way you will be more able to identify the lies in their thinking process and call it out for what it is, helping them recognize these lies for themselves.

Think about the pivotal point of my story. What happened when my parents got real and intentional about confronting my lack of confidence? What exactly did they do and how did they do it? They surrounded me with mentors who started untangling my low self-esteem. They put me in sports that gave me opportunities to excel and grow in confidence.

Thankfully, my teachers noticed my creativity and encouraged it, instead of stifling it. The sports team coaches took me under their wings. I had never felt like I was good at anything before, but in this new environment I soon found out I excelled in sports and became known as an athletic force. I was experiencing the healthy outlets of play time, sports, and arts. These role models and mentors started to address the lies that were so evident and they guided me towards the truth that I was incredibly valuable and could add value to the world around me. You can do the same for your kids as you parent intentionally, measure your words carefully, and fill your child's life with positive mentors and influencers in their areas of interest.

Today I am filled with so much gratitude for my parents because I realize just how much they had to sacrifice so I could succeed, so that I could be around first class mentors and learn in a classroom that was safe and encouraging. They did whatever it took to position me to be my best. They worked to stop the avalanche of defeat and criticism. Picking my mentors and monitoring my classroom experience, they surrounded me with adults who saw potential in me, not problems. They spoke truth, not flattery, and did their best to find the balance between confidence and arrogance. When I found martial arts, I was ready to use my life experience to live better. This led me to my life work in a field where movement and motivating others was expected and required.

My story, like yours, is filled with ups and downs. Pain and passion. Positive and negative voices and experiences. I now understand I would never have been able to create the safe place that my martial arts academy is today or even write this book if wasn't for that story. However, those lies I believed as a child have become my sworn enemy. I have dedicated my life to helping families identify when those lies are planted in their child's brain, equipping them to replace the lies with truth while they are still young. My hope is that they won't have to go down a long road of healing like I did, but rather can live as confident leaders from the start.

The Leaders for Life Formula

Sometimes we wish parenting was as simple as following a formula to get a certain outcome. Parenting just isn't that easy, though. However, I have created a formula for living a life of purpose and it can be used to guide us in leading our children. Of course, it's not really a mathematical formula, but I use a mathematical template to share it:

$$(Worth > Lie) + L4L = ID \text{ \& Purpose}$$

This formula offers a bit of a review of some of the intentional parenting strategies we've talked about already. Let's break down the formula to better understand how we help guide our kids to be leaders for life.

(Worth>Lie)

In math, we always solve what's in parentheses first. This is where we tackle our lies with truth. We set out to change our child's thinking in order to set them free from whatever lies they are entertaining. In my childhood, my parents helped me shift from "I'm dumb," to "I'm talented." It changed from "I'm a disappointment," to "I have something to offer." Both my mentors and my parents helped me know and internalize the truth, and the truth set me free.

Intentional parents recognize what lies their children are hearing from others, or worse yet, saying to themselves. They look beyond the surface and outward behavior to explore the heart and what's going on there. Resisting the urge to just address the symptoms ("You're moody today. Go to your room until you can come out happy."), they dig deeper, ("It seems like something is bothering you. Can you identify what you're feeling? Are you overwhelmed? Worried? Upset? Feeling hurt?). Then, delivered with large doses of love, they help them understand the lie that's been wounding them and gently and firmly remind their precious child of the truth. In this formula, their worth is present, ready for us to continually identify and cultivate it. And when we do, it has the incredible ability to dissolve lies.

One of the best ways to help our children learn how to overcome lies with truth is to give them space to think. Rooting out lies on our own is a deep internal process. If our schedule is packed from dawn till dusk, we won't have the time or space to contemplate what is going on in our minds. Make sure your kids have some space in their schedule to simply "be."

Creativity also helps our children develop healthy mental processes. This means allowing them time to make messes (as long as they are cleaned up properly), letting them play, and sometimes, letting them be bored until they figure out what to do. This free time forces their brains to think and create, both incredibly important skills for rooting out lies and discovering truth.

L4L: Leaders For Life

Developing leaders for life incorporates both leadership and life skills. Remember the seven C's that help us avoid parenting potholes? Children who learn and practice these skills are:

- Connected to their purpose
- Confident in their value and ability to contribute
- Compassionate towards others
- Communicators who know how to speak and listen well
- Collaborators who bring people together and find a win/win
- Critical thinkers who can analyze and problem solve on their own
- Creatives who discover unique ways to fill needs in their world

Once we've replace a lie with truth, we help develop lie-destroying habits that propel them towards becoming world-changing leaders as they grow. We can then practice and evaluate their use of these habits with goal setting. In fact that's how we bring it all together

When our child has a goal and is moving towards it, they are exercising their leadership muscles. If it's not already, help them **connect** the goal to their purpose. **Critical thinking** and **creativity** muscles are flexed as they make an action plan for achieving the goal. If they need the support of others to achieve their goal, then they are practicing their **communication** and **collaboration** skills. In fact, some of the best goals involve service and making others' lives better in some way. When they serve, they are demonstrating **compassion**. Finally, when they reach their goal, the sense of accomplishment builds their **confidence** far more than any compliment ever could!

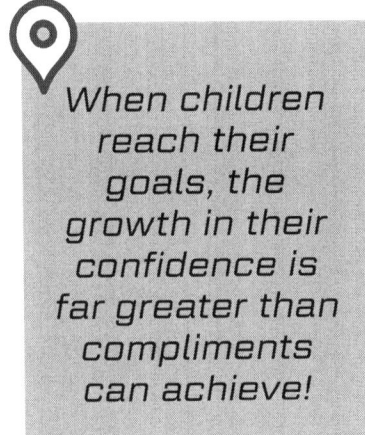

> *When children reach their goals, the growth in their confidence is far greater than compliments can achieve!*

ID: Knowing Our True Identity

Everyone of us wants to belong. I know when I was young, I desperately wanted to fit in. What would have happened if I had gone through my adolescence in the same circumstances, with the lie of my worthlessness continuing to grow at a rapid rate? Thank goodness I never had to find out. This was because my parents were intentional about helping me discover my true identity. That knowledge empowered me to walk in my own gifts and talents and use what made me unique to make the world a little better for someone else. Our gifts and talents, combined with our passions, unite to form our sense of identity, which leads us to our purpose.

Discovering and celebrating what makes your children different will actually give them a stronger sense of that identity and purpose.

I can't talk about this topic of identity without mentioning that if your child has an extreme case of identity crisis like mine, I encourage your family to pursue some professional help. I highly believe in family counselors. Their wisdom and empathy have helped me personally as well as every member of my family overcome a myriad of obstacles. Seeking professional help is a sign of strength. We certainly don't have to navigate challenges alone.

Purpose: Why We Were Put on the Planet

I once heard TD Jakes, one of my favorite pastors, say, "If you can't figure out your purpose, figure out your passion. For your passion will lead you right into your purpose." In other words, when your children discover their passions and then connect them to their gifts and talents, that intersection is where they will discover their purpose.

Too many young adults head off to college unsure of what they want to do. Off they go anyway. They study hard, change their major once or twice or more, then struggle to find a job that utilizes their hard earned school talents. If they are lucky, they find a job that aligns with what they studied. Too often, however, they wind up with a job they dislike and work there for years, all the time wondering if they are missing something. Internally they're asking questions like, *Am I supposed to be doing something else? But what?* (We won't even talk about the school debt they acquired getting them to this place!)

But what if, when our children are young, they already have a good idea of what they are passionate about? What if they already know how that passion logically combines with their giftedness and they actually pursue a purpose from an early age? They might be able to graduate from high school already knowing what they want to do with their lives! They won't hesitate and second guess their worth. They won't pursue a future that someone else gave them.

(Worth>Lie) + L4L = ID & Purpose. This is our formula for raising our children to be confident leaders who live purpose-filled lives. Defeating lies with truth plus instilling the seven leaders for life habits of success results in a strong identity and a life-giving purpose that ignites their passion. This, my friends, is how you launch a leader.

Let's Be Intentional

Having taught thousands of children over the years, I can attest that I've never found two who were ever the same. Every child is unique. Understanding their unique wiring will help you intentionally parent your incredibly talented child. Do you know your child's love language, learning style, and personality temperament? If not, take some steps to identify them today.

What Is My Child's Love Language?

Gary Chapman has a wonderful book called ***The Five Love Languages of Children.*** I would highly recommend you read it, but here is a brief summary of the concept: people receive love in different ways. For some, a hug says, "I love you" loud and clear, while a flower bouquet seems meaningless. For other people, it's the other way around. They would much rather receive the gift than the hug.

Miscommunication arises in relationships when someone who likes hugs is hugging their friend who would much rather receive a gift. One thinks they are showing love while the other feels none. Recognizing and using our child's love language is a great tool for intentional parenting. As Gary Chapman says, "Discover your child's primary language—then speak it—and you will be well on your way to a stronger relationship with your flourishing child.[4]"

Below are Gary's top five love languages. If you think one of your family members receives love in this manner, put their initials next to the language, and be intentional about communicating your love in they way they will best receive it.

1. **Words of affirmation.**
   Love compliments and recognition.

2. **Quality time.**
   Love your undivided attention.

3. **Gifts.**
   Love giving and receiving gifts.

4. **Acts of service.**
   Love when you go out of your way to serve them.

5. **Physical touch.**
   Love physical affection.

---

[4] Chapman, G. and Campbell, R. *The Five Love Languages of Children.* Chicago: Northfield Publishing, 2012. Pg. 22

What Is My Child's Learning Style?

Typically, most people learn in one of three ways:

1. Seeing (visual learners)
2. Hearing (auditory learners)
3. Feeling (kinesthetic learners)

Here are tips for identifying and teaching to your child's unique style:

Visual Learners: To fully understand, they learn through seeing things. They love watching before trying something new. Whatever lesson you are trying to teach them, be sure to demonstrate it first so they know what it should look like.

Auditory Learners: These children love listening. They like explanations and will often ask a lot of questions. Thoroughly explain things to them and encourage questions.

Kinesthetic Learners: They learn best by doing. Many children who struggle in school are challenged because they learn kinesthetically. Public education is geared towards visual and auditory learners. Walk alongside kinesthetic learners, guiding and correcting as necessary because they learn best by exploring.

Is My Child an Introvert or an Extrovert?

The main distinction between introverts and extroverts is where they gain their energy. Introverts recharge their batteries by spending time alone. Extroverts gain energy when they are around other people. Olivia's older brother is an extrovert. When he was a child, and especially when he was a teenager, he would go stir crazy if he stayed in the house too long. He had to go out and be around people. Olivia's sister is an introvert. When she was younger, her mom had to make sure she'd be able to spend a day at home after a social event because those exhausted her both physically and emotionally.

Of course, introverts cannot spend their whole lives at home. They must be encouraged to interact with others, to develop a few deep friendships. But if they talk less, have fewer friends, and prefer being at home, there is nothing strange or wrong with them. They are simply introverted. The world needs people who are quiet and thoughtful. The ideas they choose to express are incredibly valuable. In fact, introverts often notice things others don't and are able to think between the lines.

By the same token, extroverts need to come home every once in awhile to rest. They must be encouraged to spend some time doing things that are important like spending time with the family, doing homework, and contributing to household chores. Don't take their desire to socialize outside of the family personally. They're simply filling up their emotional fuel tank. The world needs extroverts because they spice things up and keep life interesting!

Use the space below (or a separate notebook) to identify each of your children's unique characteristics.

Child's Name _____

    Love Language: _____

    Learning Style: _____

    Temperament: _____

Child's Name _____

    Love Language: _____

    Learning Style: _____

    Temperament: _____

Child's Name _____

    Love Language: _____

    Learning Style: _____

    Temperament: _____

Launch a Compassionate Leader

I was devastatingly heartbroken when I heard about the death of one of our student's older sisters through the media. Reports of the incident said cause of death was alcohol poisoning when she became heavily intoxicated at a party. In my frustration of this senseless death, I shared with my black belt class how dangerous it was to party and get intoxicated. I really thought I was doing something helpful. One of the mothers who was closer to the situation was observing my class and she knew the real story. After class, she pulled me aside and told me that I had no right to use this family's situation for a "teaching moment." She questioned, "How could you tarnish their reputation? Don't you truly know them?" The realization hit me that I had just caused this family additional pain, as if the death of their daughter wasn't bad enough.

This grieving family loved and respected me and my academy. Without regard to their feelings, I capitalized on this young woman's death by jumping on my soapbox while they were still in disbelief and shock. What I also did not know was that while law enforcement was investigating the incident, the family was not allowed to speak of it at all.

I knew in that moment, she was right. I had overstepped my bounds. I soon found out that this young woman's death was not from drinking, but from being hit by a drunk driver. She hadn't been drinking, but the person who hit her had been.

I was so embarrassed and upset with myself that I didn't want to go out of my house or even be seen in public. How could I have done something so insensitive without thinking? I will never forget that moment when I was aware that my colossal error in judgment had gotten back to this precious mother and family. I had lost all respect for myself. How could I ever teach again? How could I face this black belt class again? I had slandered an innocent young woman and her family's reputation!

This grieving mother had every right to be angry and to give me a piece of her mind. Did she do that? No, she didn't. She looked at me as I apologized, and she simply forgave me. She showed me the best living example of compassion that I have ever witnessed in my life! Her compassion brought healing into a very dark place in my life and became one of the most meaningful learning experiences in my career.

When our children grow up, they will be the next leaders of society. When they are in the White House, on the Senate floor, heading up corporations, running Town Hall meetings, or teaching a black belt class, what kind of leaders will they be? Will they be defined by judgment or compassion?

> *I dream of a future where leaders are not only **strong** in their **convictions**, but also **generous** in their **compassion**.*

We all know what it's like to be led by people with personal agendas whose actions don't match their words. It's disappointing in the least and disastrous in some situations. I dream of a future where leaders are not only strong in their convictions, but also generous in their compassion.

Before they step into these grown up roles, however, they are walking around in our homes, under our own compassionate or non-compassionate influence. I believe that parents who model compassion for their children and raise them up in it are heroes in every sense of the word. Compassion is a very difficult trait to embody. Most of us experience compassion once in awhile but to embody compassion as a leader takes a special heart posture.

Clarifying Compassion

Compassion seems like one of those touchy feely emotions that you can't quite pin down. What if compassion isn't something that is hard to pin down but it is something so deep that it has to grow from within? If that's the case, how can we grow compassion in our children? Before we dive into the how, let's understand where the power of compassion comes from by answering these questions: How can we give away what we don't have? How can we measure our heart's truest intent? How can we ask our children to demonstrate compassion if they don't know its source?

First, compassion is best given from an abundant heart. When leaders feed their own souls, and show compassion to themselves, they are more emotionally, spiritually, and physically prepared to shower compassion on others. A compassionate leader sees the value in having quiet and reflective moments, friends that encourage, small groups, yoga, exercise, church, and prayer times. If we are compassionate parents, we constantly give unconditional love and it can wear us out if we don't take time to refresh ourselves. The best thing we can give others are our rested, filled-up selves that are emotionally, spiritually, and physically healthy.

Second, compassion's truest intent is to restore other people to wholeness. Our lives can sometimes feel like puzzles with missing pieces. Compassionate leadership is being those missing pieces in the lives of others. It has no hidden agenda. If we fill in those empty places and expect something in return, it's a transaction, not compassion. True compassion is a gift given freely, with absolutely no expectation of anything in return. It is a choice to enter into someone else's pain and give them what their tired hearts need most.

In my story, I needed forgiveness. That was my missing piece. That hurting mother, who could have easily been angry, resentful, or hurtful in return, instead gave me love in the form of forgiveness. She showed me a depth of compassion that I didn't know was even possible. If our places had been switched, would I have been able to give compassion so quickly and so selflessly? Her compassionate act challenged me and changed my life. *That day, that mother's face was the closest to the face of God that I have ever been.* It was a powerful experience for sure.

Finally, the source of compassion is love. When it's all said and done, love is at the root of every true leader. Love is patient, love is kind. It doesn't envy or begrudge others their blessings. It's not arrogant, and doesn't need to boast about itself. It doesn't insist on getting it's own way. Love hates wrongdoing and finds joy in the truth. Love endures through seemingly impossible situations. Because love is fully committed, it never ends. When our children grow up experiencing this kind of love, it becomes a part of their identity. It also becomes the source for them to give compassion away to others.

The crazy thing is that when love is the source of our compassion, it actually gives back to the giver. This gift is not a simple return on investment, but a bounty of blessings that come from leading out of love. Showing compassion builds bridges between two conflicting people or ideas. It's the very thing that puts people back into relationship. In my experience, that is the biggest blessing of compassion. The relationship isn't just restored to what it was; compassion gives it an upgrade to something deeper and more genuine. The compassion I felt from this grieving mother completely restored and upgraded our relationship to one of lifelong respect.

Compassion in Action

There is a very real connection between our internal heart condition and external actions when it comes to showing compassion. When we notice our children showing compassion, we can smile because we know that our child's internal thoughts and motives are healthy. However, compassion doesn't come naturally to any of us. The truth is, we're all human and tend to think of ourselves first.

Compassion requires thinking of ourselves less and others more. The good news is that if we start training our children in compassion when they are young, they are much more likely to continue walking in compassion as adults. So how can we guide our children into leading with compassion? There are three important steps.

Valuing Others

The best place to start is by teaching kids to value others. If we don't value others, compassion is contrived. Many times we see value in things based on how it impacts our lives, but the value of a person is not based on whether or not they can add value to us. People are valuable simply because they are people. They have intrinsic value. When our children see people as valuable, they will treat them with value regardless of what they look like or where they come from.

You can check your child's level of valuing others by finding out how they think about and act towards people who are different from them. Do they play with everyone? Or do they avoid the "weird" kids at school? Are they kind to others voluntarily? Are they quick to open the door for people or help carry groceries? Do they compliment readily?

When we stop judging, we can start valuing. Every person has a story. We don't know the beginning, and we definitely can't predict the ending. But the way we treat others can have a huge impact on their present and their future. Every person has unique gifts and talents. They have something to offer the world. The way we treat them will either bring them closer to this purpose or push them further away from it. When we truly value others, every word we speak and every action we take exudes kindness and encouragement.

Serving Others

When we start valuing others and noticing them, we will begin to see their needs. *Emotional Intelligence* author Daniel Goleman says that, "True compassion means not only feeling another's pain but also being moved to help relieve it." The next level of teaching compassion is helping our children understand and practice serving others. This means taking active steps to meet those needs we notice. Teaching our children to serve others not out of obligation but out of a compassionate heart will be key in them becoming outstanding leaders and citizens in this world.

Service starts by being fully present. Oftentimes when we are with the people we love, we can catch our brain wandering off and thinking about a million different things. We lose touch with the great moments that are taking place right now. But what if we began each day by asking ourselves, "What can I do for someone else today?" When we start walking around with that attitude, our mind will stay present, and we will begin to see the opportunities to serve all around us.

Seeing and serving others in need is like taking off a pair of dark sunglasses. When we teach our children to take off the "me first" glasses and to put on the "who is in need" glasses," our children can begin to notice others in need, and think of creative ways to help and serve.

Sometimes we can get so caught up in the "doing" part of life that we forget about the loving. When we serve others it is more than checking them off of a list of to-do's. It is a commitment to being with that person in order to add value to them. Mother Teresa famously said, "It's not how much we give but how much love we put into giving." When we teach service to our children, we're not talking about our children doing an excessive amount of chores. We're talking about helping our children see the world through compassionate eyes, noticing a need and sharing love by meeting it.

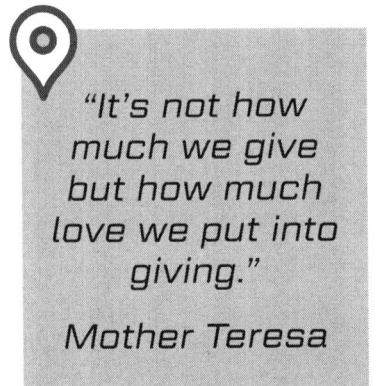

> "It's not how much we give but how much love we put into giving."
> **Mother Teresa**

Leading Others

We can also show compassion when we are leading others from a place of strength and love. You may have the impression that compassion is overtly kind, but that is not always the case.

Remember the story I shared at the beginning of this chapter? The grieving mother showed compassion by forgiving me, but the parent who pulled me aside and told me about the real situation also showed me compassion. You see, her compassion came in the form of a very difficult conversation. It was so hard to receive her seemingly harsh words of correction, but I knew she was right and I needed to hear it. Because we had that conversation, I was able to take important steps towards repairing the relationships that were broken.

Compassion isn't always just serving others, or being nice to them. It's also about loving people enough to have those hard conversations like, "I love you too much not to tell you this: _____." This is where love and leadership meet in standing up and speaking out. Donald Driver, a former football wide receiver, says, "You want a friend who's going to tell you the truth." Compassion is not controlling others, but instead caring enough to confront them. We do this all the time as parents when we discipline and correct our children out of a loving heart and not out of anger or frustration.

We also lead and show compassion when we stand up for others who cannot stand up for themselves. Our children can lead others in this way when they stand up for children who are being bullied, or make friends with the kids that are being left out. Compassion allows you to bring love to others who are hurting the most, even when you might also be hurting. True compassion is like powerful laser surgery when done from the sincerest part of the giver's heart. It's as if the laser can cut away the pain while still protecting the person.

We know that life can be painful at times and we also need to recognize that our children are watching in those painful moments. In fact, kids are excellent mirrors. Since we know this is true, let's use it to their advantage. Let's show our children what it looks like to lead a life of compassion so that they can mirror this trait to the world.

Let's Be Intentional

Teach Value

It's time for a field trip! A great way to check your child's value of others and also teach them how to value others better is to go people watching. Head out to a public place with lots of people. I would recommend the mall or a busy restaurant. Sit down in the middle of it and make observations together about the people around you. Ask your child questions to see what their heart attitude is towards others. Here are some sample questions:

- Who looks happy? Sad? Excited? Lonely? Why?
- Where do you think they might be from?
- What do you think they are shopping for? Why?
- How are they treating other people? What might have caused them to act that way?
- What might make them happier?

Teach Service

A great way to teach your children to serve is to go out as a family and serve together. Pick a community project or charity and spend a couple hours every week or month helping out. Every community has people who need help.

Here are some ideas to get your family started:

- Call your local church and find out what ways they are serving and ask where you can help.
- Contact a local charity. Some places need people to help them sort clothes or gather donations or deliver groceries to needy families.
- Walk around your neighborhood. Is there an elderly neighbor who could use help raking their yard, shoveling snow, or trimming the grass?

Teach Compassionate Leadership

Challenge your child to make friends with someone at school that they wouldn't normally be friends with. Maybe it's a kid who is always by themselves, or someone they don't like. Help your child brainstorm ways to become their friend and then put those ideas into action. Some of the strongest friendships come from the unlikeliest beginnings. But they always start with someone standing up and taking the first step and reaching out in compassion.

My husband taught a martial arts class once and challenged his students to pick one kid at school that they didn't like and become that kid's friend. The next week he asked who had completed the challenge. 5-Year-Old Johnny raised his hand. "I made Billy my friend." "How did you do it?" my husband asked, impressed. "I went up to Billy and said, Billy, you always pick on me and I don't like it and I want to be your friend. Will you come over and play today after school?" Sure enough, those two boys became great friends.

Launch an Authentic Leader for Life

Destani was born in September of 2000. Before she turned 1 year old, this country experienced an event that would forever change our lives…9/11. We didn't realize what the impact would be, however. We had no idea from that day forward we would be experiencing life from a different perspective.

Like you, I will never forget that day. It has become my generation's, "Do you know where you were on 9/11?" Whether we realize it or not, we are still feeling the effects of 9/11 on our lives and our children's lives. While the attacks on the World Trade Center and the Pentagon have had many impacts, one of the most significant results is our new "normal" for this millennium being what we might call "fear-based living".

Fast forward 8 years, Destani stood in the living room and watched the news when she was about 9 years old. There was no 9/11 being reported, but rather the everyday crimes and reports of all the things wrong in the world. After watching for awhile, she looked at me with no words. Through her stare, her body language screamed, "This is the real world that I have to be ready for?" How I wish I could have told her, "No baby, this is a horror movie."

In that moment, Destani began to think more like an adult, her childlike demeanor had become tainted with the world's realities. We can't keep her in a childlike utopia. It was at this moment in Destani's life that we were grateful we'd been training our girls from a young age to be authentic leaders for life. My husband and I couldn't shield her from her adulthood and all of life's challenges. We had the responsibility to prepare her for the world she was fast approaching and we'd actually been doing that for years.

The beauty of a child is that they don't come with fears. They don't have fear written into their DNA. They are trusting and their eyes and ears become this giant funnel for information and new experiences. The ability to learn and trust is actually instinctive in a child.

I love the university town we live in that is built around diversity. In general, our little town of around 100,000 gets along rather well. Our karate school hosts a "Parents Night Out" event once a month. This is an event that is usually on Friday night where we watch the children for a few hours so the parents can have a date night or catch up on household tasks without interruption. I love these events; it brings all the students together for a night without their parents, playing, laughing, dancing and just having fun. What the parents don't realize is this event is like an energy bar for me. It is a sea of energy and encouragement, and allows me to see through the eyes of a child...the innocence, the eagerness, the energy, and the possibilities.

Have you ever looked at life through the eyes of a child? If you do you will see their faces watching for what is right and what is "normal." You'll hear their voices ask the innocent questions about life. You'll notice their lack of prejudice because they simply don't see the color of skin or care what religion or political party people subscribe to. You'll admire their fearlessness because they're usually not afraid until our anxieties rub off on them. You'll be refreshed by their lightheartedness as they are playful and seemingly without care or concern. You'll imitate their generosity as they think everything is in abundance without limitation.

More than anything else, though, you will see them looking up to you for direction. Children are craving information and behaviors to pattern their lives after. Always inquisitive, they take and process information from every source. They are human sponges with a blank slate that is without prejudice or bias. This is why you and I need to be intentional parents who are helping to develop leaders for life.

Certainly life has a full set of its own pressures and demands. My hope is that you don't see parenting as yet another one. I hope the words of this book have given you hope and energized and encouraged you in intentional parenting. The goal you and I share is for the next generation to be well equipped to handle the challenges yet to come. They will not just survive, but thrive in it. Together we can make their future not one of fear, but a future that is full of hope, possibilities, and opportunities.

So What's Next?

It started when you picked up this book. You already made the decision to be present in your child's life. This is a bold and brave decision. However, the one that will continually need to be made several times a day will be to put down the phone and pay attention to your child, to look up from the computer and pay attention to your child, to turn off the TV and pay attention to your child, to shut off your brain and pay attention to your child.

Like the adults in their lives, what if our children turned off the TV, put down their phones, looked up from their computers because there was something more? What if we could literally put technology in its place and have it work for us?

As we go on this journey of immersing our children in a lifestyle of leadership, our own character will be transformed into the best version of ourselves while intentionally helping them become their best selves. Leadership starts with intention. Let's take hold of our children's hands and travel this road together, giving them the fantastic future they deserve.

Why You?

Why should you teach your leaders for life? Why are you qualified? It's simple. You have some understanding or desire to change your child's future. You know that change begins with active participation. The best time to start teaching is now and in your own home. No matter who we are or where we come from, we can agree that we want more for our children and the next generation.

> *The best time to start teaching is **now** and in your own home.*

You understand that a slight adjustment here and now can make a big trajectory of change for the future. Think about shooting an arrow; if you are just off a fraction of an inch, by the time it reaches the target you will completely miss the bullseye.

Play that scenario in reverse, a fraction of movement in correction now gets you closer to the target you are desiring for your children and the next generation. It's absolutely doable. Create a legacy and give the next generation the tools they need to change the world into something better for their children. This intentionality has a ripple effect over multiple generations.

Imagine a leader who envisions a future that's worth fighting for. Not fighting others, but fighting the noise of the lies that are being repeated. Imagine a leader who is creative and resourceful. One who respects others and doesn't put them down. Is compassionate, not hateful. Is ethical, not dominating. Is courageous, not fearful. Is willing to take on a risk. Not afraid to fail. Sees possibilities, not problems. Leads because the people want him or her to lead, not because of the power and accolades they will receive. This is the type of leader we need to build. Now is the best time to start, and you are the best person to help lead the charge!

The hidden bonus will be your relationship with your child. If you have committed to be this intentional about raising an authentic leader for life then your relationship with your child will probably be very deep. You are trading the sideline, crazy, hovering parenting style for one that steps into their world and shows them how to lead from the inside out. You have given them the room and love to fail. You have created an atmosphere that is conducive to raising an amazing leader and they will never hesitate about returning to because it is safe and empowering.

Our Commitment

As we come to the end of our time together, let's review where we've been and what we're committed to in the form of an agreement.

We agree as parents that:

- This vision to raise our children to be authentic leaders is possible and its time is now!
- We can disagree and still honor each other.
- Our job is to lift each other up, not tear each other down.
- We will not let anyone face a life of parenting alone.

- We are capable and up for the job! When our resolve fails, we agree to reach out to our community for encouragement.

<u>We agree as parents that we need to:</u>

- Be vulnerable, tender-hearted, and compassionate.
- Set aside our prejudices and judgments.
- Agree that our past will not hold us back for the sake of this purpose.
- Understand we don't have all the answers, and we might get it wrong at times.
- Ask for and offer forgiveness.
- Look at things from a possibility perspective.
- Use this book as a reference tool.
- Embrace the process and be authentic along the way.

You might think that changing a generation is too lofty a goal. There is a saying from an old Hebrew instruction book called "tikun olam," that says, "If you change one life, you have changed the world." Become intentional with the one or two lives in front of you and if you want to think bigger, there is always room for more.

You are not alone. It *does* take a community to raise a child. Let's make up our minds **now** to raise our children to be leaders for life.

Let's Stay Connected

Facebook: https://www.facebook.com/raisingleadersforlife/
Website: www.RaisingLeadersForLife.com

ACKNOWLEDGMENTS

From Christina

Jeff, my husband, my partner, my protector, my gift, and my love, thank you for walking hand and hand with me on this journey! Words have very little ability to capture what my heart feels about you! You have stayed focused on protecting us and our family's vision. You are my "flying rock"! Steady, grounded in God's word and faith. Our faith has pulled this project out of the grips of all the lies of "I can't do this!" into the realm of "You will, you must, and I've got you." My love and admiration for you is true and forever!

To my daughters, Melanie, Tiffany, and Destani who taught me what love is, this book is our story. Your unconditional love for our family and the students we serve is what makes me beam with pride, knowing it is from the sincerest part of who you are. All those long hours of listening to the vision of Leaders for Life is dedication in and of itself! Thank you!

To my sons-in-love, Seth and Cesar, you have a special space in my heart. You were not born to us, you chose to be in this family with open arms and an open heart willing to join us in our journey. You reveal to us our blind spots by speaking up when necessary. You always stand up for the unity we call family. I love you both and bow deeply!

To my mom and dad, thank you for introducing me to Jesus. You showed me what real commitment looks like. Thank you for sacrificing so much so that we could live a blessed life. You have been so patient in waiting 5 decades for me to mature. And let's not forget a special thanks for paying for my many years of martial arts.

To my Brazilian sister, Carmen, who is on the other side of the world, creating her leaders. My prayer is that this work gets translated into Portuguese so we can someday join forces together and see global change. A thousand kisses sent your way!

Olivia Rodriquez, you have been my co-author and voice in this project. God has intertwined our hearts, so the next generation has tools to rely on. Your wisdom is beyond your years and the grace you so freely give to all is contagious. Thank you for your friendship and partnership on this project. You humbly dedicated your time and energy to this project with no thought of your own recognition. Thanks for believing in me, believing in this project and believing in the lives it will change.

Anthony Rodriguez, thank you for sharing your wife in your first year of marriage! Thank you for doing life with us. Your character and dedication are priceless!

Kim Johnson, my most loyal friend/student/accountant. You do it all. You know all the miracles we have seen through the years. I realize it's your faith and belief in the vision that has kept us trusting in God's provision. Your friendship is priceless.

Carla, for your kingdom friendship, kingdom wisdom, and for marching with me into the unknown and bringing love into the lives we touch.

Annette, such an amazing cheerleader, idea grower, and sounding board. My favorite coach! I love you! I'm looking forward to continuing to navigate life together!

Jill Savage, your expert advice, encouragement and mining the gold in my passion helped solidify this project. Thank you.

Brandy Egli, thanks for making this happen on such a tight timeframe. Your professional, can-do attitude gave me peace of mind in the home stretch.

To my L4L family and my black belts, you are the leaders for life vision in action. Thank you for allowing me space to write this book. Thank you also for encouraging each other to create the best versions of yourselves, holding each other to a higher standard.

To my ATA family, friends, masters, and instructors, my deepest bow and respect. I not only wrote this for my students, I wrote this for yours. Your input, feedback, and encouragement throughout this project have been invaluable.

Grand Master MK Lee, for being my teaching mentor all my life. My success is due to you never giving up on me.

Mrs. Sun Lee, for keeping the vision alive and encouraging me to never forget those that can't speak up for themselves. Thank you.

To my instructors, Philip and Anne Minton, for walking me through all stages of life and leadership, seeing in me what I didn't see. You saw an orchard when I was trying to find a piece of fruit.

You helped me realize there is a potential orchard in every seed we plant.

To my Klemmer family, this book is a proof that all things are possible. We can create a world where no one is left out.

Krystal Zimmer and Kimberly Zink, for protecting and creating safe spaces for leaders to be released into our world and for believing the best in all of us!

From Olivia

I completely ditto a thank you to everyone whom Christina has expressed gratitude. In addition I would like to thank:

My husband, Anthony, for supporting and encouraging me throughout this project. You did so much so I could carve out more time to write. Not only that, but your wisdom and conviction have made this book so much stronger.

My parents, Phillip and Ramona, for teaching me about God and instilling character in me from an early age. Any wisdom I have is largely due to your influence.

ABOUT THE AUTHORS

Christina Newberry is a 7th Degree Black Belt, nationally-certified instructor who is a National Champion in the American Taekwondo Association. Christina owns and manages two Leaders for Life Martial Arts academies—one in Champaign, Illinois, and one in Houston, Texas—where she oversees the training of more than 350 students. She has always had a special place in her heart for students who were struggling. Her love for these students has led her to partner with many parents to instill confidence in their children, allowing them to become strong leaders.

Christina has been married to her husband, Jeff, for thirty years. They live just outside of Champaign, Illinois and have three daughters and two granddaughters. Christina spends her time working, writing, and dreaming big.

Olivia Rodriguez has assisted Christina in every writing project from leadership curriculum for martial arts schools, to children's church curriculum, to blogs and now books.

Olivia is currently pursuing a college degree while working part-time at Leaders for Life Martial Arts as a Manager and Instructor. She is a 3rd Degree Black Belt.

Recently married, she and her husband Anthony live in Champaign, Illinois, and plan to own and run their own Leaders for Life Martial Arts Academy one day.

Made in the USA
Middletown, DE
27 August 2023